SANDWICHES
THAT YOU WILL LIKE

Becky Mercuri

WQED
Multimedia
PITTSBURGH

WQED Multimedia
4802 Fifth Avenue
Pittsburgh, PA 15213
800.274.1307
www.wqed.org

ISBN 0-9713080-2-0
Library of Congress 2002116671
Publisher: WQED Multimedia
Project Director: Patty Walker
Project Editors: Linda Fletcher, Rick Sebak
Design: Jan McEvoy

Printed in the United States
1 3 5 7 9   10 8 6 4 2

dedication

This book is dedicated to the memory of two wonderful ladies who had a profound influence on my life: my aunt, Mona Shaw Pfarner, and my dear friend, Agnes J. Neary.

acknowledgements

Little did I know that my very first conversation with Rick Sebak, producer at WQED in Pittsburgh and creator of so many wonderful PBS shows about American food, would lead me to an exciting, in-depth exploration of America's sandwich culture. I cannot thank Rick enough for both his inspiration and for his invitation to participate in what turned out to be a fabulous adventure.

I am also deeply grateful to many others at WQED for their support, including Patty Walker for her vision, tenacity, enthusiasm, and good humor; and the WQED film crew, Buck Brinson, Bob Lubomski, Minette Seate, and Jarrett Buba, all very professional, fun, and really good at what they do. Thanks, also, to all the restaurant folks who provided a warm welcome to the film crew and who made the show and this book possible.

My special thanks and appreciation are extended to the many people who assisted with valuable information on the history of the various sandwiches, who contributed delicious recipes, or who served as guides to some of the best places to eat and enjoy America's favorite sandwiches: Pasquale "Pat" Bruno, John Thorne, Holly Moore, Chef Frank Davis, Chef David Bulla, Frank Olivieri, Chuck Taggart, Glenn Lindgren, Raúl Musibay, Jorge Castillo, Tom and Gail Weisbecker, Charlie Roesch, Robbie Mayerat, Bob Coats, Marlene Parrish, Chef James T. Ehler, Margaret Jo Borland Beckwith, Jim Porterfield, Roger Hudson, Andi Flanagan, Executive Chef Joe Castro, Donald "Dutch" Martinich, Geraldine Duncann and my friends from "Home Cooking" – you know who you are.

As always, I thank my agent, Meredith Bernstein, the best cheerleader a writer could ever hope to have. And to my husband Richard and my nephew Robbie Mayerat, I send a huge thank you for eating so many sandwiches and providing lots of valuable suggestions as I tested the recipes for this book.

foreword

To define a sandwich as two or more slices of bread with stuff stuck in between is unfair. It's not only unfair to the bread, but to the "stuff" in between as well.

To my way of eating, a sandwich is an impressive and substantial masterpiece (Dagwood was my childhood hero), the result of what happens when a creative mind smacks headlong into a love of good food.

Who among us have not fashioned a unique (and maybe even off-the-wall) sandwich master-piece of delicious delight? My creation was the elegant eggplant parmigiana sandwich that I made on Sunday nights using the leftover eggplant from our Sunday dinner at noon (in Italian households, Sunday dinner was always at noon). Our memories seem to linger on the goodness of a sandwich more than any other food.

As an inveterate student of culinary history, I am honored to be a part of this incredible book. Becky Mercuri has fashioned a Dagwood Bumstead kind of book, one that rises high, and piles layer upon layer of not only enjoyable reading but delicious sandwich ideas as well.

There is a passion for the art of the sandwich in this book; it comes across quite vividly page after page. If it is possible for a book on sandwiches to be a page-turner this is it. I suppose you could call it a riveting and ravishing experience.

And, on top of that, this book is garnished with quite a cast of characters: a notorious gambler, a frustrated Italian cook, a cartoonist, a guy named Reuben, Elvis Presley, and a sandwich invented by a Chinese cook that took on the name of a city in Colorado (Denver). This is juicy stuff.

In truth, it took me a while to get through this fascinating book. I had to stop a number of times and head for the kitchen to make this sandwich or that. In fact, before I knew it I was assembling everything I needed to make a Philadelphia cheese steak sandwich (it was so good). The next day I was back at it, but this time it was a savory Cuban sandwich, following the recipe exactly as it appears in this book. Needless to say, I stuffed myself to a fare-thee-well. And would you believe that while I was eating those sandwiches, I was reading more of this wonderful book?

In truth, this is not the kind of book you skim through and then put away never to be looked at again. I wager you will be using this book more than any other food book you have on your shelf. It has that kind of everyday appeal.

Pat Bruno

Pasquale"Pat" Bruno is the food critic for the *Chicago Sun-Times* and author of several cook-books including *The Great Chicago-Style Pizza Cookbook.*

introduction

America is a nation of sandwich eaters. We commonly live life in the fast lane, and we necessarily dote on food that is portable. The sandwich has thus become a mainstay of our existence. Sandwiches are to Americans what pasta is to Italians or what a tortilla is to Mexicans. Sandwich shops are everywhere. Take-out and delivery are not just window dressing for many such businesses; they are integral to attract and keep a loyal clientele that commonly lunches at their desks or even behind the wheels of their cars. Even when eating in restaurants, Americans love sandwiches, and not just for lunch. Sandwiches are now common offerings for breakfast, and up-scale sandwich creations are even appearing on dinner menus. In two-income households, harried parents often turn to sandwiches as a quick and convenient family meal.

Although the sandwich was invented by a notorious English gambler, John Montagu, the Fourth Earl of Sandwich, nowhere else on earth has it become so ingrained in a national cuisine. Indeed, American travelers are often shocked to find that it's seldom as commonly available abroad as it is at home.

American sandwiches have evolved from dainty offerings at afternoon tea, a custom we inherited from the English, to providing a filling and nutritious meal. Along the way, immigrants to America had a profound influence on our sandwich culture by introducing hearty sandwiches that sustained shipyard workers and shoemakers. In other cases, immigrants modified a recipe from their homeland in a way that appealed to Americans while creating a way to earn a living in their new home. Innovative cooks and chefs were responsible for introducing other unique sandwiches. In many cases, these sandwiches have become so popular that they now enjoy recognized regional or national stature. Americans everywhere are wont to talk about their favorite sandwiches with great fondness, and many affectionately refer to them as sangwiches, sandriches, sangwidges, sammidges, or sammies.

It's generally agreed that there are four basic components to a sandwich: the bread, the spread, the filling, and the garnish. While most people believe that the filling is the most important of the four, it's hard to imagine a really great sandwich without the rest, especially good bread.

You won't find fancy restaurants or haute cuisine in this book. But you will find truly great American sandwiches. And you'll find down-to-earth restaurants with character, good food, and friendly people. You'll also find recipes for some of America's greatest sandwiches, many of which have been enjoyed for decades. Several of these sandwiches have interesting stories behind their creation, and some have more than one claim as to who was responsible for their invention. The history of others has been lost in time. We've done our best to discover the true story behind each one. But with or without a bona fide provenance, these are, indeed, sandwiches that you will like.

Becky Mercuri
September, 2002

An
American
Sandwich
Timeline

It is most likely that sandwiches date back to the time when civilization and the establishment of permanent settlements occurred in the Middle East, around 9000 B.C. Grain was planted and harvested, providing the major ingredient for unleavened bread that was first baked over an open fire. Flatbreads, as they later came to be called, would have provided a natural means for conveying food from hand to mouth, holding whatever was at hand: a piece of roasted meat or perhaps some dried fish. And flatbread, as a container of sorts, allowed for ease in transporting food destined to be eaten as workers or travelers journeyed from place to place. It's entirely possible that the Biblical reference to "loaves and fishes" pointed to sandwiches that stretched the food at hand and thus fed the multitudes. According to foodwriter and culinary anthropologist Geraldine Duncann, Caesar's legions carried sandwiches on forced marches, thereby avoiding the need to stop for meal preparation. Large oval flat breads, similar to pita, were made, and when they broke camp the bread was filled with roasted meat and packed in saddlebags. Certainly, as yeast making was discovered and bread evolved into myriad forms, it became the staff of life for millions of people throughout the centuries.

According to J.J. Schnebel, an Internet researcher, the French claim that it had long been common for both travelers and field workers to carry with them meat or fish between two slices of black bread well before the English coined the term "sandwich." Perhaps the sandwich, per se, was commonly eaten by the European lower classes, whose eating habits, let alone their "recipes," were rarely, if ever, recorded in those days. And maybe it took the stamp of approval, given by the Earl of Sandwich, to make his namesake socially acceptable to the aristocracy, at least in England.

Which brings us to the "creation" of the sandwich itself. John Montagu (1718-1792), the Fourth Earl of Sandwich, is commonly credited with its invention. A notorious gambler and rogue also known as "Jemmy Twitcher," the Earl was frequently reluctant to interrupt his marathon card games and perhaps his good luck streak as well. It is said that Montagu was the first person to order sliced meat placed between two pieces of bread, an event that reportedly occurred at London's Beef Steak Club, situated above Covent Garden Theatre, in 1762. The ability to eat his sandwich one-handed left the Earl a free hand for playing cards.

America's close ties with England, even after the American Revolution, were reflected in much of our early cuisine. English colonists brought their foodways with them, and adapted their cooking in order to accommodate both New World foodstuffs and those they were able to obtain from the Old World. The few cookbooks in existence during those early years in America were mostly English imports, and even American authors tended to imitate, if not outright plagiarize, material from cookbooks written by their English counterparts.

With the publication of **Miss Leslie's Directions for Cookery** in 1837, Eliza Leslie was apparently the first person to formally introduce the sandwich to America. Born in Philadelphia in 1787, Miss Leslie spent her youth in England where she may have encountered the sandwich. Her cookbook featured the following recipe for ham sandwiches:

Ham Sandwiches
Cut some thin slices of bread very neatly, having slightly buttered them; and, if you choose, spread on a very little mustard. Have ready some very thin slices of cold boiled ham, and lay on between two slices of bread. You may either roll them up, or lay them flat on the plates. They are used at supper, or at luncheon.

By the1860s, sandwiches were commonly served as simple supper fare, and they were often packed in traveler's knapsacks. Supper, of course, was a relatively light meal since the main meal of the day, known in those days as dinner, was held mid-day.

Sandwiches, as light fare for luncheons, suppers, or picnics, continued to revolve mainly around thinly sliced ham placed between equally thin slices of bread until 1884. That was the year that Mrs. D.A. Lincoln, the first principal of the Boston Cooking School, wrote the very first version of the **Boston Cooking School Cook Book**. It became the standard by which all other cookbooks of the period were judged, and it presented more variety in sandwich fillings, including cooked ham, corned beef, or tongue; lobster or chicken salad sandwiches; and raw beef sandwiches, recommended for invalids "who could not otherwise take raw meat."

Lincoln's cookbook was followed, in 1896, by **The Original Boston Cooking-School Cook Book** by Fannie Merritt Farmer, and it actually included an entire chapter devoted to sandwiches. Both white and brown bread were recommended, and Farmer gave instructions for such fillings as sardines, anchovies, fried oysters, jelly, nut and cheese, and fruit. However, these were still not the hearty sandwiches that we know today, but dainty, fussy concoctions based on spreads and thinly carved meats. With crusts removed from bread that was often cut in decorative shapes, this was food destined for the tea tables of polite Victorian society.

During the first two decades of the twentieth century, sandwiches continued to evolve, and they were made with an ever-increasing array of fillings. Of importance is the fact that several of our most famous sandwiches were actually created by immigrants during this period, even though they would not take their place in the mainstream of American foodways for several years.

In the 1920s, technology ushered in a veritable sandwich revolution. On May 24, 1921, Wonder Bread, "the new wrapped loaf," festooned with those famous red, blue, and yellow balloons, was introduced to the American market with great fanfare. It was named "Wonder" because of its one-and-a-half-pound size. With ready-made bread generally available, Americans increased their sandwich consumption as a major part of meals, and people began referring to white bread as "sandwich bread" or as a "sandwich loaf."

Two other technological innovations ensured the success of the sandwich in America's culinary repertoire. The first pop-up toaster, called the "Toastmaster," was introduced in 1926 for use in the American home. Pre-sliced bread, first marketed by Wonder Bread in 1930, accounted for nearly 80% of bread sold in the United States by 1933, and Americans were so enthusiastic about it that the expression "the best thing since sliced bread" was coined. Clearly, both the toaster and sliced bread paved the way for the wave of sandwiches that would follow and that would be embraced by an adoring American public.

During the 1920s, luncheonettes serving sandwiches had begun popping up everywhere. There was even a popular song, "A Cup of Coffee, A Sandwich and You," released by Billy Rose and Al Dubin in 1925, which paid a kind of romantic tribute to the sandwich. By the late 1920s and the early 1930s, sandwiches had become more robust, often made from heavier breads and rolls with hearty fillings. Sold from pushcarts to hard working immigrant laborers, and fueled by the hard times of the Depression Era, sandwiches were an inexpensive but complete meal. They could be ordered at most lunch counters across the United States, and people packed them in their lunch boxes as a convenient, portable food.

The popularity of the sandwich in America was positively impacted by other technological changes as well. Affordable automobiles meant that Americans were on the move, and travelers needed to eat. This spawned the American drive-in restaurants that sprang up throughout the country. In **The American Drive-In Restaurant**, author Michael Karl Witzel recounts the story of that first successful drive-in eatery, the Pig Stand, opened in 1921 just off the busy Dallas-Fort Worth Highway. Its creator, Jessie G. Kirby, had assessed the mentality of America's car owners, deciding they were too lazy to get out and eat. And, indeed, travelers as well as locals out for a drive and a meal were delighted with the fast carhop service, the ability to eat in the privacy of their own vehicle (a special bonus for parents with small children), and the tasty sandwiches that made a great alternative to the generally below-average food that travelers had previously endured.

While the Pig Stand specialized in pork sandwiches, it wasn't long before other drive-ins with various sandwich and drink specialties appeared throughout the United States. A&W Root Beer opened its doors in 1921 in Sacramento, California, and many more such establishments, under various names, followed. The mainstay of the new road food eventually became the hamburger, accompanied by French fries, soft drinks, and milk shakes. But it was enough to firmly establish sandwiches as ultimately acceptable in the American psyche.

Although America's entry into World War II in 1941 necessarily meant rationing, the popularity of the sandwich continued. Sandwiches once again assumed their Depression Era role of providing nourishing, inexpensive, and filling meals eaten in American homes and carried off to factories by workers employed in America's essential war industry.

When the war was over, and American soldiers returned home, they brought with them a taste for foods with an international flavor. Previously scorned as "foreign food" by many Americans, sandwiches born in other cultures and countries and brought to America by immigrants were suddenly in demand. Italian Submarines, Spiedies, and Chicago's Italian Beef Sandwiches joined the lexicon of popular regional delights. Americans' increasingly sophisticated palates also provided a warm welcome for new sandwiches introduced by later immigrants, like the Cubans who fled the Castro government in the late 1950s, or like the Vietnamese who introduced the Bâhn Mi when they arrived in the 1970s, and the falafel introduced by immigrants from the Middle East. And as Americans traveled throughout the country, they discovered other regional favorites such as Beef on Weck from Buffalo, New York; New Orleans' Po-Boys; California's French Dip; and Chicken Fried Steak Sandwiches from Texas. Today, in many instances, these and other major American cities are identified with a special sandwich indigenous to the area.

The Wheat Foods Council declared 2002 "The Year of the Sandwich," honoring its creation 240 years previously by John Montagu, the Fourth Earl of Sandwich. This clever public relations strategy clearly recognized the importance of America's sandwich culture. As the council pointed out, Americans eat more than 45 billion sandwiches per year, with the average American consuming 193 sandwiches annually. With new sandwiches continually being introduced and embraced by an adoring public, America is clearly in the throes of a "sandwich explosion."

2

Old Favorites: Sandwiches for Kids of all Ages

Peanut Butter & Jelly

For centuries, ground peanuts have been used in cooking. Scholars report that they were incorporated into stews in fifteenth century Africa, and many claim that it was probably Negro slaves who first popularized the use of ground peanuts in American cooking. But it took many years before their valuable commercial potential was exploited.

Although the original creator of peanut butter is still disputed, one story claims that food manufacturer George A. Bayles was persuaded by a St. Louis physician, in 1890, to process and market peanut paste, a source of protein that could be easily eaten by people with such bad teeth they couldn't chew meat. Joseph Lambert of Battle Creek, Michigan, is also credited with the invention of peanut butter. Then, in 1904, a vendor named C.H. Sumner introduced peanut butter at the Louisiana Purchase Exposition in St. Louis. By 1908, Columbus, Ohio-based Krema Products, among other purveyors, was selling peanut butter, but because it was packed in barrels and spoiled so quickly, company owner Benton Black sold his product only within the state. By 1922, peanut butter and its distribution had been revolutionized with a new churning process developed by Joseph L. Rosenfeld of California. Peanut butter was not only smoother, but because it was stabilized, it could be kept on the shelf for up to a year. Swift & Company made early use of the new process and renamed their E.K. Pond Peanut Butter to Peter Pan around 1928. A reported dispute between Rosenfeld and Peter Pan lead to his launch of rival Skippy, and in 1932, Rosenfeld added chopped peanuts to his creamy base, creating the first crunchy-style peanut butter. The broad distribution of pre-sliced bread dovetailed with the increasing popularity of peanut butter, but the addition of jelly to the sandwich doesn't seem to have appeared before the early 1940s.

During World War II, Americans became accustomed to peanut butter and jelly. Food was rationed, especially butter and meat, and peanut butter was promoted as a source of protein for soldiers at the front as well as those back on the home front. Because both peanut butter and jelly were included in United States military rations, some speculate that American soldiers may be responsible for combining the two ingredients between slices of bread, perhaps because jelly made it easier to eat the sticky peanut butter. By the close of the war, peanut butter was a kitchen staple, and with the end of sugar rationing, Welch's Grape Jelly, sold in grocery stores since 1923, became its choice companion. Today, Proctor & Gamble operates the world's largest peanut butter plant where some 250,000 jars of Jif are produced daily.

Peanut butter statistics tell an interesting story. With some 700 million pounds of it consumed annually in approximately 75% of American homes, it's obviously a favorite food. And the average American child is said to consume 1,500 peanut butter sandwiches prior to high school graduation.

Sandwich

Peanut butter has formed the basis for some unique sandwiches, such as the fabled peanut butter and sauerkraut on raisin bread favored by Laverne De Fazio, a character played by Penny Marshall in the ABC sitcom *Laverne & Shirley*. Dedicated Elvis Presley fans still honor "the King" by making his favorite sandwich, fried peanut butter and banana, which Elvis ate with a knife and fork. (An interesting recipe in the 1940 edition of **Ruth Wakefield's Toll House Tried and True Recipes** indicates that guests at the Toll House in Whitman, Massachusetts, enjoyed sandwiches with peanut butter and banana long before Elvis made it famous.) Some folks swear that there's nothing better than peanut butter and bacon sandwiches. But most Americans favor the old standby, peanut butter and jelly, usually grape, on white bread.

Fried Peanut Butter and Banana Sandwich

2 slices white bread, lightly toasted
3 tablespoons smooth peanut butter
½ medium ripe banana, peeled and coarsely mashed
2 – 3 slices bacon, fried crisp and drained (optional)
2 tablespoons butter

Spread peanut butter on one slice of the toasted bread and cover it with the mashed banana. Add bacon if desired. Top with the second slice of toast. In a medium-sized skillet, melt the butter and add the sandwich. Fry over medium heat until golden on both sides, turning only once. Cut sandwich into squares and serve hot. Yield: 1 sandwich.

Where to Go:

Located in New York's West Village, Peanut Butter & Co. is likely to take you back to kindergarten – or at least to your school lunch box days. With bright yellow walls as the backdrop, peanut butter sandwiches are enjoyed by one and all. The sammies are good-sized, made of freshly baked white or wheat bread, and upon request they'll cut off the crust for you just like Mom did. Diners choose from six types of peanut butter made fresh every day. Selections range from the classic PB & J to all sorts of fun options like Fluffernutter®, the Elvis with bananas and honey, grilled, and a peanut butter BLT made with toast and bacon. Naturally, all sandwiches come with potato chips and carrot sticks.

The menu at Elvis Presley's Memphis Restaurant features many of Elvis' favorite dishes, including the fried peanut butter and banana sandwich. In this rendition, billed as the "original," the bananas are sliced rather than mashed.

Peanut Butter & Co.
240 Sullivan Street
New York, NY

Elvis Presley's Memphis Restaurant
126 Beale Street
Memphis, TN

Bologna (BALONEY, BOLOGNY)

Whether one says bologna or baloney, this popular American smoked sausage, typically made of pork and beef, is sliced and served as sandwich meat. It's named after the Italian town of the same name where the original or real bologna, called mortadella, was created. According to Root and de Rochemont, authors of **Eating in America**, bologna is likely an American attempt to reproduce mortadella but with the spiciness greatly reduced.

Although bologna has been around for many years, the folks at Oscar Mayer Foods may well deserve credit for its wide popularity. Most Americans of a certain age recall "The Oscar Mayer Bologny Kid" who sang about the glories of Oscar Mayer bologna in the famous ad campaign created by J. Walter Thompson in 1975. Statistics reveal that Americans annually consume 800 million pounds of bologna. And Oscar Mayer claims that every year, we eat approximately 2.19 billion bologna sandwiches, a figure that translates to 6 million per day or 69 sandwiches every second.

Sandwiches

While mortadella comes in several different varieties, Americans typically eat only one style of bologna, thinly sliced and served on white bread. Differentiation comes with the choice of condiment: mustard, mayonnaise, and butter are the top three contenders. Sometimes, bologna is fried and served on a roll, with or without fried onions. For something a bit more exotic, Americans whip up a batch of bologna salad sandwich filling.

Old Fashioned Bologna Salad Sandwich

2 cups finely ground German bologna
½ cup finely ground sweet pickles
½ medium onion, finely ground
2 teaspoons regular prepared mustard or Creole mustard
⅔ cup mayonnaise
8 bulky-style rolls
Lettuce

In a medium bowl, combine bologna, pickle, onion, and mustard. Mix well. Place a lettuce slice on the bottom of each roll and top with ½ cup bologna salad. Cover with other half of roll, slice, and serve. Yield: 8 sandwiches.

Ham

The ham sandwich is the earliest sandwich mentioned in American cookbooks, and according to industry statistics, it's still the most popular sandwich in America today. The ham sandwich has retained its leading title for several years, beating even pizza and hot dogs.

In the United States, there are an infinite variety of ham sandwiches from which to choose. And Americans can be pretty picky about their ham. According to Chef James Ehler's website, www.foodreference.com, some folks want their ham only from the left leg of the pig, considered more tender than the right leg which is used by the pig for scratching, and which creates tougher meat. Others prefer hams produced in certain locales, like Smithfield ham that is produced from peanut-fed hogs in the Smithfield, Virginia, area, or the salty country cured hams from the area surrounding Cadiz, Kentucky.

Then, of course, there are the "ham look-alikes" such as SPAM™ (SPAM is a registered trademark of Hormel Foods LLC for luncheon meat) and Underwood Deviled Ham. The Underwood Company, established in Boston by Englishman William Underwood as a condiment business in 1822, produces the latter. Around 1868, the Underwood Company began experimenting with a mixture of ground ham and spices in a process they called "deviling," and they adopted the famous red devil logo that was patented in 1870. It's the oldest trademark still used in the United States today. The popularity of Underwood Deviled Ham as a sandwich filling seems never to have waned since it was introduced nationally around 1895.

SPAM, manufactured by the Hormel Company, is a luncheon meat made from chopped ham and spices. Originally introduced in 1927 as Hormel Spiced Ham, the threat of competitors who were cloning the product inspired the company to hold a contest in order to devise a unique name. In 1936, the winning name of SPAM was chosen, a combination of "sp" for spiced and "am" for ham.

SPAM went off to war with American troops in the 1940s and became a staple of the military diet. Although GIs made endless jokes about SPAM at the time, they developed a taste for the luncheon meat, and when they returned home after the war, sales boomed. By 1945, a billion cans of SPAM had been sold, and it still retains its popularity as the number one canned ham product in the United States. SPAM is so celebrated that it is the guest of honor at festivals like Austin's SPAM Cookoff and Olympics held annually on the Sunday closest to April Fool's Day.

Sandwiches

Underwood's Deviled Ham is used as a sandwich filling for both tea and hearty luncheon

Where to Go:

Lea's Lunchroom on Highway 71 South in Lecompte, Louisiana, is as famous for its dough-baked hams as for its homemade pies based on cherished family recipes. Established in 1928 and still run by the same family, Lea's is a Louisiana Hall of Fame Restaurant. Ham is served with plate lunches and it's also sold by the pound for take-out. Lea's also ships over 67,000 pies a year to loyal fans in the United States and abroad. In honor of the historic restaurant, the town of Lecompte has assumed the title of "Pie Capital of Louisiana" and holds an annual Pie Festival in October.

Need A Quick Fix?

Smithfield hams can be ordered at http://www.smithfieldcollection.com

Kentucky country hams are available from the following purveyors:

Balance Country Hams
Route 1, Box 15
Oakland, KY 42159
(270) 563-3956

Broadbent's Hams
6321 Hopkinsville Road
Cadiz, KY 42211
Telephone: (800) 841-2201
or (270) 235-5294

sandwiches. In the early 1900s, it was a substitute for bacon or ham in Eggs Benedict, one of the first breakfast sandwiches in America. Eggs Benedict was such a popular dish by 1912 that Underwoods developed a recipe that also substituted cream sauce for hollandaise and used it in their advertising. SPAM, a popular luncheon meat for sandwiches, is generally used as a substitute for ham or bacon and has been used to create innumerable sandwich specialties based on many regional favorites in the United States, such as the Reuben, Monte Cristo, and the club.

Ham lunch meat and sliced baked ham are popular items at restaurants and deli counters throughout the United States, and both are used to create an enormous variety of hot and cold sandwiches in home and commercial kitchens. Some of the most popular include ham and cheese (plain or grilled) and ham salad.

Cheese

In **The American Century Cookbook**, author Jean Anderson says she believes the popularity of the American grilled cheese sandwich had its origins in cheese canapés served in the late nineteenth century when grated cheese was sprinkled on small rounds of bread or thin crackers called zephyrettes and baked until bubbly. Other food authorities believe that the grilled cheese sandwich is most likely based on France's *croque monsieur*, a toasted sandwich filled with ham and cheese. (A *croque madame* is a *croque monsieur* served with an egg on top.)

By 1923, **The Boston Cooking-School Cook Book** by Fanny Farmer featured "Dream Sandwiches," which were cheese sandwiches browned in butter. With the Depression years, meals and entertaining became simpler, often centered on family style food prepared at the table in a chafing dish. This became known as the "Sunday Night Supper," and Welsh rabbit (or rarebit), composed of cheddar cheese melted in ale, seasoned with cayenne or Worcestershire sauce, and served on toast, was a popular entrée. It wasn't long before "Cheese Dreams," cheese sandwiches cooked in butter in a chafing dish, also became popular. They most likely hearken back to Fanny Farmer's "Dream Sandwiches." Open-faced cheese dreams often featured the addition of sliced tomato or crisp bacon strips.

Those first cheese sandwiches have spawned many American variations over the years. According to Kraft Foods, Americans eat more than 4.07 billion Kraft® Singles, a popular sandwich cheese, every year. That equates to 129 slices per second. And that's only the beginning when it comes to tallying up the figures related to America's cheese sandwich consumption.

In diner lingo, which serves as a kind of shorthand, a grilled American cheese sandwich is called a GAC, sometimes also called a "jack" due to the pronunciation of GAC, and a grilled cheese with bacon sandwich is called a Jack Benny after the famous radio and TV comedian.

Sandwiches

There are seemingly endless combinations for cheese-based sandwiches, beginning with the cheese itself followed by variations in the bread, additional fillings, and the spread. Some are old-fashioned concoctions while others utilize new and creative ingredients. Everyone, it seems, has his or her favorite. Here's an old diner specialty that has maintained its popularity.

Open-Faced Grilled Cheese, Bacon, and Tomato Sandwich

2 slices of white bread, toasted

Thinly sliced sharp cheddar cheese sufficient to cover each slice of bread
6 slices of bacon, crisply cooked and drained
2 large slices of tomato

Preheat broiler. Generously cover each slice of toast with cheddar cheese, and broil just until cheese melts. Remove from broiler, and top each with 3 slices of bacon. Place tomatoes on top of the bacon, and return to the broiler until tomatoes are heated through and the cheese begins to brown on the edges. Yield: 1 serving.

Bacon, Lettuce & Tomato

Bacon has long been a staple of American kitchens due to the large consumption of pork in this country. In the United States, bacon is typically made from cured and smoked pork bellies. Production totals more than 2 billion pounds annually, and much of it is used in the preparation of that all-American sandwich, bacon, lettuce, and tomato. With the rapid growth of supermarkets after World War II, fresh lettuce and tomatoes became available year round, a factor which lead to the increased popularity of this sandwich in the past fifty years.

Diner lingo long ago termed this sandwich the "BLT," and the acronym has been part of our language for years. According to Chef James Ehler of www.food reference.com, the BLT is the second most popular sandwich in the United States (ham is number one).

Sandwiches

A BLT is typically composed of crisp-fried bacon, sliced tomato, and iceberg lettuce on white bread (sometimes toasted) that's spread with mayonnaise. Here's a relatively recent combination said to originate in California.

The BLTT
(Bacon, Lettuce, Tomato, and Turkey)

4 slices of good quality white bread, toasted
Mayonnaise to taste
2 large leaves of iceberg lettuce
1 small avocado, mashed or sliced
¼ cup crumbled blue cheese
2 large slices of tomato
½ pound thinly sliced roasted turkey
6 slices crisply cooked and drained bacon

Spread mayonnaise to taste on one side of each slice of toast. Lay out two slices of the toast, and cover each with a large leaf of lettuce. Divide the mashed avocado and the crumbled blue cheese and layer on top of the lettuce. Top each with a slice of tomato, half of the sliced turkey, and 3 pieces of bacon. Cover the sandwiches with the remaining slices of toast, cut in half, and serve immediately. Yield: 2 sandwiches.

Chicken & Egg Salads

When it comes to chicken or egg salad sandwiches, one is tempted to wonder which came first: the chicken or the egg. Fannie Farmer first mentioned both chicken and egg salad in the 1896 edition of **The Original Boston Cooking-School Cook Book**. Because scholars claim that cookbooks of this period typically lagged several years behind what was actually being served, one might assume that the transformation of salads into sandwich fillings probably occurred some time after the Civil War. Certainly, various salad combinations were attractive fillings for the popular tea sandwiches served during the latter part of the nineteenth century. By 1885, the great hotels of New England, serving as a refuge for

Eastern city dwellers escaping the heat, offered Victorian-style high tea service in their tea rooms, most likely fueling the development of ever more elegant sandwiches for high society.

Over time, chicken and egg salad sandwiches became heartier, and it wasn't long before they appeared on restaurant luncheon menus or showed up in lunch boxes. Recipes for chicken and egg salads are presented as substantial sandwich fillings in a delightful volume entitled **The Up-to-date Sandwich Book: 400 Ways to Make a Sandwich** compiled by Eva Greene Fuller and published in 1909. In more recent years, Paul Simon memorialized the chicken and egg salad sandwich in his song "Mother and Child Reunion."

Sandwiches

Today, both chicken and egg salad sandwiches remain American favorites, and like so many of our original combinations, they are likely to appear all gussied up with new ingredients that enhance both flavor and appearance. While the debate over mayonnaise versus various other dressings rages on, one thing is for sure: most folks have definite preferences for one or the other, usually based upon what they ate as children, and it isn't likely they're going to change those preferences any time soon.

The late Bert Greene, a well-known cookbook author, created a recipe for chicken salad that was said to duplicate a popular dish sold at Balducci's, a gourmet grocery and take-out food shop in New York City. The following was inspired by Bert's recipe, but it's much simpler to make.

Chicken Salad with Tarragon and Artichokes

3½ cups cooked chicken breast,
cut into 1-inch cubes

1¾ cups quality mayonnaise
1 cup finely chopped celery
½ cup finely grated fresh carrot
½ cup finely chopped red bell pepper
2 teaspoons dried tarragon
½ teaspoon dried oregano
Salt and freshly ground black pepper to taste
1 14-ounce can artichoke hearts packed in water,
drained and coarsely chopped

6 white or whole wheat pocket pita breads,
cut in half
Lettuce
Sweet red pepper strips for garnish (optional)

Combine all ingredients for chicken salad. Cover and refrigerate at least 4 hours to allow flavors to blend.

Line each side of the pita bread halves with a lettuce leaf. Fill pockets with chicken salad, and garnish with red pepper strips if desired. Serve immediately. Yield: 6 sandwiches.

Note: Twelve mini pocket pita breads may be substituted for the large size.

Santa Fe Chicken Salad Sandwich
Reprinted with permission from Bob Coats, Wellsville, New York.

Chicken:
6 chicken legs
Water
1 tablespoon paprika
1 tablespoon ground black pepper
2 tablespoons salt
1 tablespoon chile powder
1 tablespoon garlic powder
1 tablespoon onion powder
1 teaspoon cayenne

Chicken salad:
8 green onions, finely chopped
2 stalks celery, finely chopped
2 large cloves garlic, finely chopped
½ cup plain yogurt
½ cup mayonnaise
1 tablespoon spicy brown mustard
1 tablespoon brown sugar
1 teaspoon chile powder
Salt and pepper to taste
Cooked chicken (see above)

Butter spread:
½ cup butter, softened
1 teaspoon smoked salt
1 teaspoon ground black pepper
1 teaspoon chile powder

Mayonnaise spread:
½ cup mayonnaise
¼ cup Miracle Whip
1 teaspoon garlic powder
1 teaspoon brown mustard

16 slices tomato-parsley bread or bread of choice
Romaine lettuce
Thinly sliced tomatoes

Chicken: In a large pot, cover chicken completely with water. Add spices, and simmer for one hour. Remove from heat, cover, and refrigerate in broth over night. Next day, skim off any fat, drain chicken, and discard the skin. Remove chicken from bones and coarsely chop it.

Chicken salad: Combine all ingredients except chicken, mixing well. Add chicken and mix. Cover and refrigerate for at least one hour or until ready to use.

Butter spread: Combine all ingredients, mixing well.

Mayonnaise spread: Combine all ingredients, mixing well.

To assemble sandwiches: Spread 8 slices of bread with butter mixture. Top with lettuce, chicken salad, and tomato slices. Spread remaining slices of bread with mayonnaise mixture and place over filling. Slice each sandwich in half and serve immediately. Yield: 8 sandwiches.

Turkey

While roast turkey may be the centerpiece of our traditional American Thanksgiving dinner, there are plenty of folks who confess to a preference for leftovers from the big feast – especially turkey sandwiches. According to the National Turkey Federation, the number one way to use Thanksgiving leftover turkey is in sandwiches. The lucky folks in Newark, Delaware, don't have to wait for the big day to enjoy a great turkey sandwich. Capriotti's Sandwich Shop has customers lined up at lunch time for their signature sandwich called the Bobbie, made with turkey, stuffing, and cranberry sauce.

For those who can do without stuffing, the following sandwich will make short work of Thanksgiving leftovers.

The Best Part of Thanksgiving Turkey Sandwich

Cranberry sauce:
1 fresh, seedless, unpeeled orange, washed and quartered
1 pound fresh cranberries, washed, drained and picked over
¾ cup sugar

For each sandwich:
Two slices of quality white bread
2 tablespoons cranberry sauce or to taste
1 large slice lettuce
Thinly sliced roasted turkey to taste

Cranberry sauce: **Combine all ingredients in a food processor, and process until mixture resembles a slightly chunky sauce. Place sauce in a bowl, cover, and refrigerate at least 4 hours to allow flavors to develop. Leftover sauce may be frozen.**

To assemble sandwich: **Spread cranberry sauce on both slices of bread. Layer lettuce and turkey on one slice of bread, top with the second slice of bread, cut in half, and serve immediately.**

Yield: 1 sandwich.

Where to Go:

Capriotti's Sandwich Shop, 614 Newark Shopping Center, Newark, Delaware, serves Thanksgiving-style sandwiches all year round.

Chicken

Domesticated in Asia some 4,000 years ago, chicken was brought to America by Columbus. While it has always been popular here, chicken was not always affordable to everyone. When Herbert Hoover became President of the United States in 1929, he vowed that Americans would have "a chicken in every pot and a car in every garage." Unfortunately, Hoover was confronted with the ravages of the stock market crash and the ensuing Great Depression, and he was unable to live up to his vow that served only to underscore economic conditions of the time.

The phrase "chicken every Sunday" had always signified a comfortable standard of living, if not wealth, sought by most Americans. But it wasn't until after World War II that chicken became affordable to people other than the most affluent. Indeed, this ideal was reflected in a popular 1948 movie entitled *Chicken Every Sunday* that starred Celeste Holm.

Today, chicken is not only affordable but it has increased in popularity, leading all meats in per capita consumption at more than 80 pounds per year. Most people cite its availability, versatility, taste, and ease of preparation as reasons for increased purchase.

Sandwiches are the perfect venue for chicken, which is easily and tastefully combined with a large variety of spreads and other filling ingredients. Consumers can buy chicken from the deli section of the supermarket or use leftover roast chicken. Smoked chicken has become very popular in recent years, delivering an added dimension of taste as exemplified in the following recipe. For the best quality, buy a whole smoked chicken and carve it into thin slices for use in sandwiches.

Southwest Smoked Chicken Sandwich
Andi Flanagan of Moose Pass, Alaska, is a genius when it comes to preparing smoked meats, poultry, and fish. Her popular recipe for chile mayonnaise is reprinted with permission.

Chile Mayonnaise:
½ cup good quality mayonnaise
¼ teaspoon ground cumin or more, to taste
1 fresh jalapeno pepper, seeded, deveined, and finely chopped
½ cup chopped fresh cilantro

4 fresh hoagie rolls
Chile mayonnaise (above)
Lettuce
1 pound thinly sliced smoked chicken
8 thin slices of tomato
Thinly sliced red onion to taste

Chile Mayonnaise: In a small bowl, combine all ingredients for chile mayonnaise. Cover and refrigerate for at least two days to allow flavors to develop.

Preheat broiler, then lightly toast the hoagie rolls. Remove rolls from broiler and spread chile mayonnaise on the inside of each roll. Layer each sandwich with lettuce, 1/4 pound smoked chicken, 2 slices of tomato, and sliced red onion. Cut each sandwich in half and serve immediately. Yield: 4 sandwiches.

Tuna Fish

Tuna salad sandwiches are enormously popular in the United States and date, like so many others, from the early twentieth century when housewives typically made small tea or luncheon sandwiches from the mixture. In those days, people favored sandwiches made from a variety of fish and seafood ranging from lobster, shrimp, salmon, and crab to oyster, caviar, shad-roe, and sardines. Tuna was first canned in 1903 when an experimental shipment of 700 cases of albacore was shipped out from California. It was practically an overnight success, and by the 1920s, other species like skipjack, bluefin, and yellowfin were also being canned.

As sandwiches became heartier concoctions, so did the tuna fish sandwich. Popular with children and teenagers, instructions for a tuna sandwich were given as "Flaked Fish Sandwiches" in the various editions of the **Young America's Cook Book: A Cook Book for Boys and Girls Who Like Good Food,** first published in 1938.

Sometime around the 1960s or 1970s, the "Tuna Melt" was created. Jean Anderson, in **The American Century Cookbook**, says that the inventor may have been a college coed with a toaster oven in her dormitory room. Word of the "Tuna Melt" spread quickly, and it was so popular that it eventually became a standard offering on restaurant menus throughout most of the United States.

Sandwich
Tuna salad recipes vary enormously, with most prepared in accordance with the preferences of the individual cook. They typically include tuna fish, mayonnaise, chopped onion, and chopped celery. Sometimes, chopped green pepper or chopped hard-boiled egg is added. The filling is spread between two slices of bread, which may be toasted, and the bread ranges from plain white sandwich bread to whole wheat, rye, or even San Francisco sourdough. Open-faced tuna salad sandwiches on which slices of cheese, usually American, have been placed are broiled until the cheese melts, resulting in the "Tuna Melt."

In the late 1950s, school cafeterias introduced the "Tuna Bunstead," a sandwich comprised of basic tuna salad, chopped hard-boiled egg, and chunks of cheese packed into a hot dog roll and baked until hot and the cheese is melted. Although no explanation of the word "bunstead" could be found, it's fun to theorize that it's a take-off on the name of comic strip character Dagwood Bumstead.

Today, the tuna sandwich has gone up-town in some of our trendiest restaurants where a fresh tuna steak is broiled and served in sandwich form. Both the tuna salad sandwich and the tuna melt are ubiquitous items on lunch menus of restaurants throughout the country. In diner lingo, the tuna salad sandwich on toast is called a "radio," which is a pun on "tuna down," just as one would "turn down" a radio. Tuna sandwiches, of course, are also a perennial favorite in school children's lunch boxes as well as on school lunch menus.

Tuna Bunsteads Circa 1958

18 ounces water-packed, chunk light tuna fish, drained and flaked
½ cup finely chopped celery
½ cup finely chopped onion
1 hard boiled egg, chopped
1 heaping cup of cubed Velveeta cheese
⅓ cup mayonnaise or just enough to combine and moisten the ingredients
½ teaspoon salt
Ground black pepper to taste
10 hot dog rolls

Preheat oven to 350°. Place all ingredients except rolls in a medium bowl, and mix just enough to combine. Fill the hot dog rolls, and wrap and seal each one individually in foil. Place filled, wrapped rolls on a baking sheet, and bake for 15 – 20 minutes or until filling is piping hot and cheese has melted. Yield: 10 sandwiches.

Note: Serve tuna bunsteads with potato chips just like they did in the school cafeteria!

Club Sandwich

Gambling in men's social clubs during the latter part of the nineteenth century provides an interesting connection with those same activities enjoyed by the Earl of Sandwich back in 1762. The location, however, was Saratoga Springs, New York, not London.

In 1870, John Morrissey, a retired prizefighter and New York City politician, built an ornate Italianate structure, somewhat incongruously called the Club House, that became the premier gambling establishment for well-heeled Easterners making their summer escape to Saratoga Springs. In 1894, the business was sold to Richard Canfield, "America's Greatest Gambler" and operator of several other casinos, at various times, in New York City and Rhode Island. A noted art collector, Canfield renamed it The Casino and brought a new sense of elegance by adding Tiffany windows, paintings, sculpture, and Italian gardens.

But perhaps more importantly, at least from a culinary perspective, Canfield added a dining room that served nothing but the finest of cuisine to the high stakes rollers allowed to enter those private, hallowed halls. And here it was, according to legend, that the gambler's buffet was invented along with the club sandwich, designed to provide delicious nourishment to gamblers who, like the Earl of Sandwich before them, wanted to minimize their time away from gaming pursuits. It's also said that the potato chip, originally called the Saratoga Chip, was born in The Casino's kitchen. Word of the club sandwich spread quickly, making it a popular item throughout other gentlemens' social clubs and perhaps explaining the original name, "Clubhouse Sandwich."

Jean Anderson, in **The American Century Cookbook**, points out that the earliest printed recipe she could find for the club sandwich was an entry in the 1902 **Woman's Favorite Cookbook** by Ann R. Gregory and 1,000 Homemakers, in which the club sandwich was attributed to Gunther's in Chicago. Gunther's was a candy manufacturing business owned by Charles Gunther, with the factory located at 212 State Street and the confectionery located on Wabash Street.

While this is an interesting counter-claim, it should be noted that public pressure against gambling, as well as the consumption of alcoholic beverages, was continuing to mount at the turn of the century. It was that same public pressure, which manifested itself in the Temperance Movement, that resulted in Canfield's closing of The Casino in 1907. And, despite the popularity of the club sandwich, it's likely that no cookbook author or publisher of the day would credit a gambling operation with its creation. Attributing it to a candy shop was surely more acceptable, and this may well explain the honor given to Gunther's.

The Temperance Movement may also explain the claim that the club sandwich was developed for service in railroad dining or club cars during the seventy-five years comprising the Golden Age of railroad travel that began in 1868. This attribution unfortunately lacks specific reference to any particular railroad company or contracted operator of dining cars that might have developed the sandwich. James D. Porterfield, author of **Dining by Rail** and a noted authority on railroad dining cars and cuisine, says that he researched volumes of material related to food served in din-

ing cars of the period, including some 7,500 recipes, and to date, he has been unable to substantiate the claim that the club sandwich was developed for use in the railroad industry. While most dining cars of the late nineteenth century and early twentieth century served elaborate meals, it wasn't until several years after the club sandwich was introduced that it began to appear on menus found in the dining, club, and buffet cars of first class trains.

Sandwich

Food scholars continue to debate the actual construction of the original club sandwich as it pertains to the number of bread slices used. In his 1972 work, **American Cookery**, James Beard roundly criticized the addition of a third slice of toast, declaring that the resulting "three-decker" club was not at all authentic, to say nothing of palatable. Beard's directions for an "authentic club sandwich" consist of two slices of buttered toast, mayonnaise, sliced chicken breast and peeled tomato, a bit of salt, crisp bacon, a bit more mayonnaise, and a second slice of toast.

Beard's instructions are apparently well founded if one limits consultation only to specific cookbooks that contain recipes for the club sandwich using two slices of toast, such as the 1909 **Mrs. Curtis's Cookbook: A Manual of Instruction in the Art of Everyday Cookery** by Isabel Curtis and the 1916 **Salads, Sandwiches, and Chafing Dish Recipes** by Marion H. Neil. However, Fuller's **The Up-to-date Sandwich Book** from 1909 provides an interesting comparison. Recipes for a number of club sandwiches, including those for the Sheridan Park Club, the Colonial (Club) Sandwich, the Country Club Sandwich, the Chicago Club Sandwich, and the Turkey Club Sandwich all call for three slices of bread, and not all of them call for the bread to be toasted.

Interesting is the recipe for the Saratoga Sandwich, which consists not only of three slices of bread but calls for a layer of fried oysters with horseradish followed by one of chicken and fried bacon.

Today, a club sandwich is not considered as such unless it's a three-decker, and although Beard decried the substitution of turkey for chicken, standard choices include chicken, turkey, and ham – or some combination thereof. Even more modern additions to the classic club range from avocado (the California Club) to spinach, cucumber, and alfalfa sprouts with a range of choice in bread, sometimes not even toasted.

Where to Go:

Although the club sandwich is offered on thousands of restaurant menus throughout the United States, devotees may want to visit its purported birthplace, now the home of the Historical Society of Saratoga Springs, New York.

The Casino
Congress Park
Saratoga Springs, NY

3

The Dagwood
Launches a
Host of "BIG"
Sandwiches

The Dagwood

We owe the Dagwood sandwich to Murat "Chic" Young, the cartoonist who created the comic strip "Blondie" in 1930. Blondie Boopadoop, originally portrayed as a flighty girl of low social status, eventually married Dagwood Bumstead and became a practical-minded housewife. Today, Blondie more closely resembles American women of our time – she's a housewife who also runs a catering service.

But it was Dagwood who created the first big sandwich that became his namesake. In the late 1930s, Blondie fans saw Dagwood, clad in his famous polka-dot pajamas, grab some bread, throw open the refrigerator, and begin piling on the ingredients for what would become the most famous sandwich of all time. Today, the Dagwood Sandwich is featured on many restaurant menus throughout the United States, and it is even listed in **Webster's New World Dictionary** as "a thick sandwich with a variety of fillings, often of apparently incompatible foods," most certainly a legacy of Dagwood's refrigerator raids.

Sandwich

The comic strip "Blondie" ultimately left the composition of the Dagwood sandwich up to the reader's imagination, and when creator Chic Young authored **Blondie's Cook Book** in 1947, he left plenty of room for individual improvisation in his sandwich recipe. Called the "Skyscraper Special," typical Dagwood ingredients include layers of sardines and cold baked beans along with suggestions for other components of the sandwich. **Blondie's Cook Book** was reissued in 1996, with new illustrations by Dean Young, son of Chic Young. The recipe for the "Skyscraper Special" remains unchanged.

The Dagwood Sandwich

To make a proper Dagwood, open the refrigerator and combine whatever basic sandwich ingredients take your fancy. Then add any or all leftovers.

Where to Go:

Blondie's Home of the Dagwood
Universal Studio's Islands of Adventure -
Toon Lagoon
Orlando, FL

Hoagie, Hero, Submarine, Italian Sandwich, Grinder, Spuckie, Bomber, Torpedo, Rocket, Wedge, & Zeppellin

Big American sandwiches, modeled on the Dagwood, based on long Italian rolls or French bread, and made to order from a vast array of ingredients, are known regionally under various names. In 1967, Edwin Eames and Howard

Robboy listed thirteen different names for these sandwiches in their paper entitled "The Submarine Sandwich: Lexical Variations in a Cultural Context." In some cases, the history, or at least the legendary origin, of these sandwiches has been documented. In other cases, little or nothing has been recorded, and we are left to wonder how each sandwich was named.

The hoagie seems to be the earliest of these sandwiches. During World War I, ships were built in the Philadelphia area known as Hog Island. Italian immigrant workers in the shipyards there, working long double shifts, regularly lunched on enormous sandwiches filled with cold cuts, lettuce, onions, tomatoes, and peppers. According to the Pennsylvania-based Wawa Food Market chain, a man named Al DePalma ended up at Hog Island looking for work during the Depression. When he spied the shipyard workers wolfing down those sandwiches, DePalma's first thought was that they looked like a bunch of hogs. DePalma wasn't one to let an opportunity pass, and instead of continuing his job search, he opened a luncheonette, specializing in those same big cold cut-filled sandwiches that he called "hoggies."

By the late 1930s, DePalma had partnered with Bucelli's Bakery, introducing an eight-inch roll that has since become the standard for today's hoagies. With the advent of World War II, DePalma literally created a hoggie factory in the back of his restaurant in order to meet the demand for his sandwiches from round-the-clock shipyard workers. Around 1945, the "hoggie" became known as the "hoagie." It's believed that the sandwich may have been renamed in honor of the great American composer Hoagland Howard "Hoagy" Carmichael.

Today, hoagies are the "Official Sandwich of Philadelphia," and every summer, Wawa Food Markets sponsors Hoagie Day as part of Philadelphia's annual Welcome America celebration. The huge hoagie built to feed the crowd around City Hall gets bigger and bigger each year; the hoagie in 2001, stuffed with meats, cheeses, and garnishes, measured some 10,000 feet in length.

No such detailed history has been uncovered for sandwiches of this type that are known by different names, so perhaps they all evolved from the hoagie as it migrated to other parts of the United States. Of interest is the fact that so many of the names, like submarine, bomber, and torpedo, carry a military connotation.

The term hoagie is used mainly in Pennsylvania and New Jersey while hero, a word dating to around 1955, is used in New York City. Italian sandwich is used in the Northeast, especially Maine, and grinder is used chiefly in New England in the states of Massachusetts, Rhode Island, Connecticut, and Vermont. Spuckie is an old Boston term for a big Italian-style sandwich. Then there are submarines, said to date from the 1960s, a term so common and widespread that it cannot be assigned to any particular region. Other terms include rocket, bomber, wedge, zep or zeppelin, and torpedo. And in the Midwest and from mid-Tennessee to the Alabama Gulf Coast, Dagwood is still a popular term of reference.

Sandwich shops and restaurants throughout the United States commonly offer submarine-type sandwiches. The popularity of these sandwiches has spawned numerous chains that specialize in them.

Sandwich

By whatever name, America's big sandwiches are based on crusty Italian rolls or French bread that contain layers of meat, cheese, and lettuce garnished with a choice of tomatoes, onion, pickles, and/or peppers. Meats typically include a choice of ham, roast beef, salami, turkey, and capicolla, while cheeses include American, Swiss, and provolone. The sandwiches are dressed with oil, mayonnaise, and/or mustard. The original cold cut sandwiches have evolved into increasingly wider varieties that include hot offerings based on items like meatballs or sandwich steaks.

And now, there are even vegetarian versions of hoagies like those at Chickie's Italian Deli in Philadelphia. This place is one of sandwich sleuth Holly Moore's greatest finds (see http://www.HollyEats.com). First of all, Chickie uses what's said to be the best hoagie bread in Philly on which to build his stupendous sandwiches. The "Original Veggie Hoagie" is really something: baked eggplant, sautéed greens, roasted peppers, and sharp provolone cheese. Chickie also makes a "real" tuna hoagie based on tuna meat rather than tuna salad. And then there's the "Chickie Special:" prosciutto, sopressato, dry cured capicolla, sharp provolone, roasted peppers, lettuce, tomato, and onions. It doesn't get much better than that.

Where to Go:

Chickie's Italian Deli
1014 Federal Street
Philadelphia, PA

Po-Boys & La Médiatrice

Po-Boys

Although the po-boy (aka poor boy) sandwich of New Orleans is frequently included in the same classification as hoagies, submarines, and others of that genre, it is, in reality, a sandwich that presents itself in some truly unique variations that set it apart from the rest of the pack.

As is the case with so many of our favorite sandwiches, there is more than one story about the origin of the po-boy, but it's likely that the following account is accurate. According to New Orleans food writer and restaurant critic Tom Fitzmorris, the po-boy was created by Bennie and Clovis Martin, owners of Martin's Poor Boy Restaurant, as a way to help striking streetcar workers during the 1920s. The Martins loaded French fries into the long loaves of French bread, added roast beef gravy that contained scraps of meat, and sold it for a nickel to the men on the picket lines. In an interview with Denise Gee for **Coastal Living**, John Demers, New Orleans native and food editor of the **Houston Chronicle**, also credits the Martin Brothers for the creation of the po-boy, and he further notes that this explains the curious, but much loved, French fry po-boys still offered by some New Orleans restaurants today.

La Médiatrice

A variation on the po-boy is New Orleans' famous oyster loaf, also known as La Médiatrice or "the peacemaker." Food historians report that it originated during the late nineteenth century when all of America was crazy about oysters. Husbands who had been carousing all night in the French Quarter would bring oyster loaves home in the hope of pacifying their jealous wives. The oyster loaf was also known during this time in other cities, such as San Francisco, where it is said that it was created at Mayes Oyster House, established in 1867. But nowhere has the oyster loaf retained its popularity like it has in New Orleans.

Sandwiches

Chuck Taggart, whose web site www.gumbo pages.com provides some of the most definitive information available on Louisiana food and cooking, addresses the po-boy at great length. According to Taggart, an authentic po-boy requires very fresh po-boy-style French bread that, alas, is rarely available outside New Orleans. Baked in brick ovens by long-established bakeries, this is a loaf characterized by its crisp exterior and feathery-light interior. One is advised to substitute the best quality French bread available.

For oyster loaves, oysters sautéed in butter and perhaps enriched with a bit of heavy cream are placed inside a hollowed-out loaf that has been buttered and lightly toasted in the oven. Alternatively, the oysters may be lightly breaded with cornmeal and deep-fried. Other popular variations today include oysters coated with a lemony garlic-butter sauce or barbecued oysters, which, in New Orleans, means oysters fried in a peppery butter sauce.

Popular po-boy fillings include roast beef, shrimp, ham, Creole hot sausage, hamburger, and yes, even French fry po-boys doused with roast beef gravy. The venerated Mother's Restaurant has long been known for its excellent po-boys, especially the Ferdi Special, a combination of Mother's famous baked "black ham" (due to the caramelized glaze), roast beef, and what is known in New Orleans as "debris," a rich roast beef gravy that includes pieces of the beef that have fallen off as the roast cooks. It's also available with cheese (Swiss cheese is popular), whereupon it becomes a Ralph (Ferdi was the brother of the original owner and Ralph was Ferdi's son). In recent years, even deep-fried po-boys have been introduced at some of New Orleans' hottest eateries.

In New Orleans, it's crucial to know the local "lunch counter lingo" when ordering a po-boy since the inevitable question arises as to whether or not the sandwich is to be "dressed." The choices are two: "dressed" means the sandwich will be prepared with mayonnaise (pronounced "mynez"), pickles, lettuce, and tomato. The other choice, in the local vernacular, is "nuttin' on it." Mother's deviates a bit from the norm by dressing their po-boys with shredded cabbage, pickles, mayonnaise, and both yellow and Creole mustards.

Parasols, established in the 1950s smack in the middle of the Irish Channel district, is housed in a building that dates to 1902 and is famous for its St. Patrick's Day celebrations. It's also famous for roast beef po-boys with deep, rich gravy, but for many customers, nothing hits the spot like one of Parasol's fried shrimp or oyster po-boys. Encased in cornmeal breading, the seafood is fried to a golden turn and heaped into warm, crispy French bread.

The legendary Acme Oyster House, established in 1910, also serves up fried seafood po-boys along with its unique hot pepper-based mayonnaise, lettuce, and tomato. At Liuzza's, a neighborhood restaurant that dates back to 1947, patrons often wait their turn to enjoy fried seafood po-boys composed of soft shell crab, oysters, or shrimp while others opt for an original style po-boy made with French fries and gravy.

And then there's Domilise's, an old fashioned, storefront-style po-boy shop in New Orleans' Uptown residential area that's a favorite among locals. Established in the 1930s, it's still owned by the Italian-American Domilise family, and many of the employees have been there for upwards of thirty years. Most folks go there for the hot sausage po-boy covered with beef gravy or the golden brown, deep-fried shrimp and oyster po-boys.

But beware: these po-boy joints are only the tip of the iceberg when it comes to enjoying New Orleans' famous sandwiches. Even some of the locals have trouble deciding on a favorite, and they venture throughout the Crescent City, checking out a host of selections and endlessly debating the quintessential po-boy.

Creole Roast Beef for Po-Boys

This recipe was given to Chuck Taggart by Wendy, "a good Metry girl." Chuck says that it must be made with homemade beef stock to get the true taste, and he's right! Reprinted with permission from Chuck's web site www.gumbopages.com

1 5-pound beef shoulder roast or beef brisket
¼ pound piece of salt pork, sliced into ¼-inch strips
6 - 8 cloves garlic, minced and divided
3 cups minced onion, divided
1 tablespoon salt, divided
1 teaspoon ground black pepper, divided
¼ cup lard, bacon drippings, or solid vegetable shortening
1 tablespoon Creole seasoning blend (recipe follows)
6 small carrots, diced
6 ribs celery, diced
1 tablespoon minced fresh parsley
2 – 3 sprigs fresh thyme
1 cup good quality red wine
3 quarts boiling beef stock (recipe follows) or more, if needed
2 beef marrowbones
Salt and pepper to taste
Pinch or two of cayenne (red) pepper (optional)

10 to 12 9-inch po-boy rolls or French baguettes
Garnish:
Mayonnaise
Lettuce
Tomatoes
Pickles

Cut a pattern of even incisions across the top of the roast every couple of inches, each long and deep enough to hold a slice of salt pork. Combine half the garlic, 1 cup of the onion (mince this finely), ½ teaspoon of the salt, and ½ teaspoon of the black pepper. Push the mixture into the slits that have been made for the salt pork, then press the salt pork into the beef. Tie the meat securely, keeping the shape of the roast as uniform as possible for even cooking.

In a pot that is broad and deep enough to hold the roast with room to spare, melt the lard over medium heat. Brown the roast on all sides, keeping the salt pork inside the slits in the meat. Add remaining garlic, onion, salt, and pepper plus carrots, celery, parsley, and thyme to the pot. Cook over medium heat until onions are limp. Add wine and enough boiling beef stock or water to nearly cover the beef, reserving extra stock. (If you substitute water for the beef stock, it won't be nearly as rich as when beef stock is used.) Add marrowbones. Cover pot and simmer over low heat for 4 hours, or until beef is very tender. Add more stock if necessary to keep beef almost covered.

Remove beef from pot and place on a deep platter that will catch and hold the dripping juices. Raise heat under the pot and boil hard, uncovered, about 45 minutes. While boiling down the gravy, baste the roast so it doesn't dry out. Strain the gravy, season it to taste with salt, freshly ground black pepper, and a small pinch or two of cayenne (optional). There should be about one quart of gravy.

Remove salt pork strips from beef and slice it as best you can (it will fall into chunks and shreds; the smaller you shred it, the more it'll be like the legendary "debris" from Mother's Restaurant). Remove any fat, bone, or gristle and discard. Place beef in a large bowl, and pour gravy over it. The resulting mixture should be sloppy, luscious, and profoundly beefy.

Serve on fresh, crisp-crusted New Orleans-style French bread or baguettes. The bread should be crispy on the outside and light on the inside but not chewy. Serve po-boys dressed (with mayonnaise, lettuce, tomatoes, and pickles) or with "nuttin' on it," but "mynez" (mayonnaise) really is a must. Yield: 10 – 12 good-sized po-boys.

Chuck Taggart's Creole Seasoning
Reprinted with permission from Chuck Taggart's web site www.gumbopages.com

2 tablespoons onion powder
2 tablespoons garlic powder
2 tablespoons dried oregano leaves
2 tablespoons dried sweet basil
1 tablespoon dried thyme leaves
1 tablespoon ground black pepper
1 tablespoon ground white pepper
1 tablespoon cayenne (red) pepper
1 tablespoon celery seed, crushed
5 tablespoons sweet paprika (Hungarian is recommended)
2 – 4 tablespoons salt (optional)

Combine all ingredients in a food processor and pulse until well blended or mix well by hand. This recipe can be easily doubled or tripled, and it makes great gifts.

Note: Chuck says that while most Creole seasoning blends contain salt, he prefers to separately control the salt content in cooking. Therefore, the salt in this recipe is provided as an option, including quantity, which can be adjusted according to taste.

Brown Beef Stock
Reprinted with permission from Chuck Taggart's web site www.gumbopages.com

8 pounds beef bones, including knucklebones, trimmings, etc., sawn into 3- 4-inch pieces
Vegetable oil
3 ounces tomato paste, thinned with
2 tablespoons water
6 – 7 quarts cold water

Mirepoix:
8 ounces onion, coarsely chopped
4 ounces carrots, coarsely chopped
4 ounces celery, coarsely chopped

Sachet d'epices:
3 or 4 parsley stems, chopped
1/2 teaspoon thyme leaves
1 bay leaf
1 whole clove
1/2 teaspoon cracked black peppercorns
1 clove garlic, crushed

8 ounces tomatoes, quartered

Preheat the oven to 400°. Lightly oil a sheet pan with sides and place it in the oven to heat. Place bones on the pan and roast for 30 minutes, turning them occasionally. Paint the bones with a thin layer of the thinned tomato paste, and roast for an additional 30 minutes, turning occasionally, until bones are evenly browned.

Place bones in a large stockpot and cover with 6 – 7 quarts of cold water. Bring to a boil, reduce heat, and simmer. Periodically skim off any scum that forms on the surface during the cooking process.

Meanwhile, drain and reserve the fat from the baking sheet. Deglaze the baking pan with water and add it to the stockpot. Continue simmering the stock for a total of 6 or 7 hours, skimming as needed. If necessary, add more water to keep the bones completely covered.

In a frying pan, toss the mirepoix with the reserved fat and brown it over medium heat. Place the ingredients for the sachet d'epices into a four-inch square of cheesecloth and tie it securely into a sack. Add the browned mirepoix, the sachet d'epices, and the tomatoes to the pot. Simmer for another 1 to 2 hours.

Strain the stock through a large strainer or china cap lined with cheesecloth. Transfer the stock to a container large enough to hold it, and refrigerate the stock overnight. The next day, skim off all the fat that has risen to the surface. The stock is now ready to use. Keep it refrigerated for up to 3 days or freeze for future use. Yield: About 1 gallon of stock.

Where to Go:

The following are all in New Orleans:

Domilise's
5240 Annunciation Street

Mother's Restaurant
401 Poydras Street

Parasol's
2533 Constance Street

Ye Olde College Inn
3016 S. Carrollton Avenue

Franky and Johnny's
321 Arabella

Casamento's Restaurant
4330 Magazine Street

Johnny's Po-Boys
511 St. Louis

Acme Oyster House
724 Iberville Street

Liuzza's
3636 Bienville Street

The Muffaletta (Muffuletta)

While most people think of the Creole and Cajun influence on the food of New Orleans, the Italians, too, have made a deep impact upon the cooking of Southern Louisiana. Italian immigrants, especially those from Sicily, arrived in significant numbers during the 1880s and 1890s. Many had been employed in the citrus trade in Italy, and they found work on Louisiana's plantations. Others settled in the French Quarter and became involved in the food industry, opening grocery stores, bakeries, and food processing plants.

It is said that Italian workers employed at the markets in New Orleans would commonly scoop broken olives from barrels and add them to the round loves of bread they brought for lunch. The loaves were called "muffs," and sandwiches with the addition of olives were eventually called muffalettas. One of those early immigrants was Signor Lupo Salvadore who, in 1906, established the now famous Central Grocery in New Orleans' French Quarter. Salvadore is credited with the creation of what he called the "muffuletta." He apparently took note of what the workers were eating, embellished it a bit, and sold made-to-order sandwiches from his grocery.

Bartolomeo Perrone, who came from Palermo, Sicily, established Progress Grocery, a long-time competitor of Central Grocery, in 1924. (Progress Grocery was sold in 2001, and the business now operates under the name of Luigi's Fine Foods.) Progress, too, claims to have invented the muffaletta. It was, as the story goes, a relative of the old Progress Grocery family who first baked muffaletta bread in New Orleans sometime around 1895. (Of interest is the fact that muffaletta bread is still made in at least one old-fashioned neighborhood bakery in Piano degli Albanese, near Palermo, Sicily, home of an Albanian colony since the fifteenth century.) So, one might say that the families of both Progress Grocery and Central Grocery had a direct hand in the creation of the muffaletta sandwich, which apparently boasts a combination of Italian and Albanian heritage.

Today, the muffaletta is on the menus of numerous New Orleans restaurants, and it is one of the city's signature sandwiches. Virtually no tourist visits the Big Easy without trying one, and many folks grab a few extra to enjoy on the plane trip home.

Sandwich

The key to a great muffaletta sandwich is in the bread, the use of fresh, premium cold cuts, and the olive salad that's included as a garnish. The bread is prepared in ten- or twelve-inch rounds and topped with sesame seeds. Since it seems to be made only in New Orleans, a common substitute is a round of crusty Italian bread.

Called "the Holy Grail of sandwich fillings" by Chuck Taggart, author of the popular Internet site http://www.gumbopages.com, olive salad is absolutely crucial to the muffaletta. Without it, you won't have the real thing. Some versions, like that sold at Luigi's Fine Foods, contain cauliflower and carrots in addition to the traditional ingredients.

The bread is sliced in half, and layered with very fresh, high quality cheese and cold cuts: thinly sliced mortadella (Italian salami), ham, Genoa salami, mozzarella cheese, and provolone cheese. A healthy addition of olive salad crowns the filling that is then capped with the top of the loaf. The sandwich, because of its size, is typically cut into quarters for serving.

The Muffaletta (Muffuletta)

1 10 to 12-inch round muffaletta bread or crusty Italian bread
¼ pound thinly sliced mozzarella cheese
¼ pound thinly sliced provolone cheese
½ pound thinly sliced Genoa or hard salami
½ pound thinly sliced mortadella sausage
½ pound thinly sliced baked ham
1 to 2 cups olive salad, to taste (recipe follows)

Optional:
½ pound thinly sliced capicolla
1 cup oregano onions (recipe follows)
Extra virgin olive oil

Bring all ingredients to room temperature before assembling the sandwich. Preheat oven to 350°. Slice the loaf of muffaletta or Italian bread in half horizontally, place on a baking sheet, and heat in oven for 5 minutes or until lightly toasted.

Remove bread from oven. Evenly distribute slices of mozzarella cheese on the top half and evenly distribute slices of provolone cheese on the bottom half. Return bread to oven and bake for 5 to 7 minutes or until cheese is softened but not melted. Remove from oven. On the bottom half, layer the meats, beginning with the Genoa or hard salami, then the mortadella, the capicolla (optional), and finally, the ham. Press down lightly on the meats to create a level surface and spoon on the olive salad. Add oregano onions and drizzle with more olive oil if desired. Cover with top half of bread, slice into quarters, and serve immediately. Yield: 4 sandwiches.

Note: Capicolla and oregano onions are a non-traditional but delicious addition to the muffaletta sandwich.

Olive Salad

1 10-ounce jar pimiento-stuffed green olives, drained and chopped
3 garlic cloves, minced
2 tablespoons drained marinated cocktail onions
2 large celery stalks, halved lengthwise and thinly sliced
1 tablespoon drained capers
1½ teaspoons dried oregano
½ teaspoon ground black pepper
1½ tablespoons red wine vinegar
3 tablespoons olive oil

Combine all ingredients in a medium bowl and stir well. Cover and refrigerate for at least 4 hours to allow flavors to blend. Bring to room temperature before using. Mixture may be stored for up to two weeks if kept in a tightly covered container and refrigerated. Yield: about 2 cups.

Oregano Onions
Reprinted with permission from **Too Good To Be True** by the late Chet Beckwith of Baton Rouge, Louisiana - a fantastic cook and dear friend who is sorely missed.

2 medium onions, thinly sliced
1 teaspoon dried oregano
¼ cup extra virgin olive oil
½ cup apple cider vinegar

Separate onion rings and place in a medium bowl. Add remaining ingredients and mix well. Cover and let stand at room temperature for an hour or two. For longer storage, refrigerate, tightly covered. Bring to room temperature before using. Oregano onions are an excellent garnish for muffalettas and po-boys. Yield: About 1½ cups.

Where to Go:

The following locations are in New Orleans, LA:

Central Grocery
923 Decatur Street

Luigi's Fine Foods (formerly Progress Grocery)
915 Decatur Street

Nor-Joe Imports
505 Frisco Avenue
Metairie, LA

Need a Quick Fix?

No time to make your own muffalettas? Don't despair. The world famous sandwich can be shipped to you straight from New Orleans. Take your pick of Central Grocery or Progress Grocery. Although the latter no longer exists, having been bought by new owners who operate under the name of Luigi's Fine Foods, the Perrone family sells its products by mail order under the name of Progress Grocery. Both firms sell muffalettas as well as olive salad. Muffaletta bread and a full range of Italian cold cuts are available from Progress. And while you're at it, complete your meal by ordering up some of New Orleans' famous Zapp's Potato Chips.

Central Grocery
Telephone: (504) 523-1620

Zapp's Potato Chips
Telephone: (Toll free) 1– 800-HOT-CHIP
Web Site: http://www.zapps.com

Progress Grocery
Telephone: (504) 455-FOOD or (toll free) 1-866-455-3663
Fax: (504) 455-3660
Web site: http://www.progressgrocery.com

Báhn Mi (aka the "Vietnamese Sub")

A relative newcomer to the American sandwich scene is the "Vietnamese sub," or báhn mi, which reflects the influence that one of America's most recent immigrant groups has exerted on our sandwich culture.

The báhn mi is based on mini French baguettes (baguettine), an inheritance from the French colonial period in Vietnam. (Food writer Kate Heyhoe notes that the báhn mi baguette is made with both wheat and rice flour, resulting in a much lighter loaf and a crispier crust.) According to a post on the Internet's Chowhound site, bread isn't native to Vietnam where it was always considered to be food for the poor who could not afford rice. During French colonial days, sandwiches made from these baguettes were sold in expensive food shops catering to the French colonists and to "French wannabes" for whom it became a status symbol in the 1940s and 1950s. These sandwiches almost always included mayonnaise, raw green onion, and whatever an individual might order for the filling.

It wasn't long before imitations of the sandwich, called báhn mi tay, made their appearance in stores catering to the Vietnamese. The xe báhn mi, literally translated as "vehicle selling bread," sold from boxes mounted on tricycles, soon followed. This last version was cheaper and essentially more Vietnamese, because it primarily featured inexpensive ingredients like cucumber, green pepper, pickled vegetables, and herbs much loved by the Vietnamese people.

By the 1960s, the original French sandwiches eaten by the colonials had pretty much disappeared from Vietnam along with the French themselves. Following the Vietnam War and reunification of Vietnam under the Communists, thousand of Vietnamese fled their homeland with many coming to the United States. These immigrants brought with them the báhn mi, and it soon made its appearance in Vietnamese sandwich shops that they established throughout the country.

Sandwich

The báhn mi is an explosion of flavors and contrasts that has caught the fancy of the American sandwich-eating public. Some aficionados, unclear as to the actual content of the sandwich, simply describe it as "filled with strange and wonderful things."

Fresh baguettes are typically toasted or heated, then filled with ingredients such as pickled daikon, carrot, and hot peppers, along with onion, cucumber, and cilantro. A choice of meat, ranging from barbecued pork, cured ham, chicken, or Vietnamese bologna, is accompanied by pâté (usually pork or chicken liver). Finally, a dressing of Vietnamese hot chili sauce or soy sauce and vinegar delivers additional punch to this tasty and exotic sandwich. It should be noted that some Vietnamese sandwich shops in the United States do serve báhn mi with mayonnaise that is either spicy-sweet or that has a vinegary bite to it.

In his food letter **Simple Cooking**, John Thorne, one of America's most celebrated food writers, presents a wonderful essay entitled "Báhn Mi and Me" in which he describes both his discovery of this exotic sandwich and his subsequent mission to uncover how it is made. We thank John for sharing with us the fruits of his labor.

Báhn Mi

Reprinted with permission from *Simple Cooking*, the food letter written and published by John and Matt Thorne (http://www.outlawcook.com).

The Bread: This can be an entire French (or Italian) light crusty roll or a wedge cut from a bâtarde (the next bread size up from a baguette). If it's not fresh from the bakery, heat it for 5 minutes in a warm oven before making the sandwich.

The Spread: Choose one or more of the following: mayonnaise, hot sauce, pork or chicken liver pâté, sweet butter, Maggi seasoning, a drizzle of nuoc cham (see recipe below). I like pâté spread on one side and nuoc cham mixed into mayonnaise on the other.

The Topping: Consider these mandatory: thinly sliced European cucumber, marinated slivers of daikon and carrot or carrot alone (see recipe below), and lots of fresh coriander. Optional extras include sliced jicama, a few basil or mint leaves, some slivers of scallion (or very thinly sliced onion), and slices of fiery hot chile pepper.

The Filling: One or more different kinds of Vietnamese cold cuts (look in the freezer section of your Asian grocery), preferably from a pork loaf (white) and a cured ham (pink). A reasonable supermarket substitute would be a few slices of chicken loaf and boiled ham. Those leery of cold cuts in general might try thin slices of roast pork, grilled mushrooms, or slices of firm tofu, drained and then marinated in nuoc cham overnight.

Nuoc Cham
(Vietnamese Dipping Sauce)

1 clove garlic
1/2 teaspoon ground chile paste
1 Thai chile pepper, seeded (optional – see note)
2 tablespoons fish sauce (see note)
1 tablespoon fresh lime juice with pulp
1/3 cup hot water
2 tablespoons sugar

Put the garlic, chile paste, and optional Thai pepper into a mortar or food processor and pulverize into a paste. Combine this mixture with the rest of the ingredients in a small bowl and stir until the sugar has dissolved. This sauce can be kept in the refrigerator for one month. Yield: 3/4 cup.

Cook's Note. Thai chile peppers are small and intensely hot. Any small fiery (or not so fiery!) chile pepper can be substituted. Fish sauce, nuoc mam, is an essential element of Vietnamese cuisine. It is made by packing anchovies in salt and drawing off the brine; the best brands contain no other ingredients. Apply with a light hand.

Cu Cai Carot Chua
(Carrot and Daikon in Vinegar)

1 medium carrot
1 small daikon (sweet white radish)
1 cup water
2 teaspoons rice vinegar
2 teaspoons sugar
1 pinch salt

Peel the carrot and radish and cut each into 2-inch lengths. Either grate coarsely into long strands or, with a sharp knife or vegetable peeler, cut each length into paper-thin strips. Put the rest of the ingredients in a small bowl and stir until the sugar completely dissolves. Marinate the strips of carrot and radish in this mixture for at least 1 hour or as long as overnight. Remove the vegetables from the liquid before using. If marinated carrots alone are preferred, omit the daikon and cut the marinade proportions in half.

Where to Go:

Huong Lan Sandwiches
1655 Tulley Road
San Jose, CA
Other locations in Milpitas
and Sacramento, CA

Ba Xuyen
6011 Seventh Avenue, Sunset Park
Brooklyn, NY

Saigon Banh Mi
88 East Broadway Mall, Unit # 108
NY, NY

An Dong
5424 8th Avenue
Brooklyn, NY

New Thanh Huong Sandwich
1156 Story Road
San Jose, CA

Vietnam Sandwiches (aka Discount Deli)
426 Larkin
San Francisco, CA

Saigon Sandwich Shop
560 Larkin
San Francisco, CA

4

Famous
Regional
American
Sandwiches

Ask someone what their favorite sandwich is and you may well be able to tell where they are from. That's because so many well-known American sandwiches are actually popular, regional specialties.

WHAT'S YOUR BEEF?

From plain old hamburgers to fancy open-faced steak sandwiches, Americans love their beef. So it's no wonder that many of our most famous regional American sandwiches feature it. Although United States beef consumption had been on the decline for nearly two decades, 1999 saw a reversal of that trend, and in 2000, per capita beef consumption was at 69.5 pounds. According to www.beeffoodservice.com, beef sandwiches placed first and second in tracking of the fastest growing sandwiches and accounted for almost fifty percent of all sandwiches sold in commercial restaurants in 2001.

Philadelphia Cheese Steak

According to legend, the Philadelphia cheese steak sandwich was born one day in 1930 at Pat Olivieri's hot dog stand, located at the Italian Market in South Philadelphia. Longing for something different, Olivieri cooked some thinly sliced beef and onions on his hot dog grill and piled it all into an Italian roll. As the story goes, a cab driver that regularly patronized the hot dog stand came by just as Pat was eating his new creation and asked for one, too. Upon tasting it, the cabbie immediately advised Pat to forget about hot dogs and to sell his beef sandwich instead.

In the 1940s, cheese was added and somewhere along the line, Olivieri, with no competition from other vendors, declared himself "King of Steaks." Pat's only location in South Philly is still operated by the same family. It's a place where communal ties remain strong, and everyone's proud of the fact that Sylvester Stallone, also a South Philly native, filmed scenes for his first *Rocky* movie in the neighborhood.

Framed by more neon lights than you could ever imagine, Geno's Steaks, another popular spot for Philadelphia's favorite sandwich, is just across the street from Pat's. And these aren't the only spots for Philly's famous sandwich. As the city's cheese steak war rages on, everyone claims to have "the original."

Sandwich

The Philadelphia Cheese Steak Sandwich is composed of very thinly sliced and grilled beef and onions (rib eye steak is commonly used), hot Cheez Whiz® (the most authentic), American cheese, or, more recently, provolone cheese and, usually, a garnish of fried hot or sweet peppers, all piled into a crusty Italian roll. Some cheese steak emporiums chop the steak up on the grill as it cooks, creating an interesting melding of meat, onion, and cheese. Fried mushrooms, garlic, and ketchup are optional, and more recent additions include lettuce and tomato.

The Original Pat's King of Steaks Philadelphia Cheese Steak Recipe
Reprinted with permission from Pat's King of Steaks.

1 large Spanish onion, coarsely chopped
6 tablespoons soya bean oil
Cheese: Pat's recommends Cheez Whiz® –
American or provolone works fine
24 ounces thin sliced rib eye or eye roll steak

4 crusty Italian rolls
Optional:
Sweet green and red peppers, coarsely chopped and sautéed in oil
Mushrooms, coarsely chopped and sautéed in oil

Heat an iron skillet or a non-stick pan over medium heat. Add 3 tablespoons of oil to the pan, and sauté the onion to desired doneness. Remove the onion Add the remaining oil to the skillet, and sauté the slices of meat quickly on both sides. Melt the Cheez Whiz® in a double boiler or in a microwave oven.

Place 6 ounces of the steak into each roll. Divide the onion among the rolls, and top with hot Cheez® Whiz. Garnish as desired with peppers, mushrooms, and ketchup. Put on the theme song to the first **Rocky** movie and enjoy! Yield: 4 sandwiches.

Note: Steak can be sliced thinner when it is partially frozen.

Where to Go:

The following locations are all in Philadelphia:

Pat's King of Steaks
1237 E. Passyunk Avenue

Geno's Steaks
9th and Passyunk

Dallessandro's Steaks
Corner Henry Avenue & Wendover

The French Dip

French immigrant Philippe Mathieu created the French Dip in 1918. This momentous event took place at his sandwich shop, Philippe the Original, which he established in 1908 in downtown Los Angeles. As the story goes, Philippe accidentally dropped a French roll into the roast pan drippings as he was making a sandwich for a hungry policeman. The policeman soon returned with several friends in tow, all requesting that their sandwiches be "dipped" as well.

According to the current owners of Philippe the Original, it is not known if the now-famous sandwich was named the "French Dip" because of the French roll used to make the sandwich, Philippe's French heritage, or because the name of the police officer was French.

However it came about, the French Dip is recognized throughout the United States, and at Philippe's, it's said that over 5,000 people come through the doors on a daily basis in search of the real thing. While that might indicate long waits in most restaurants, efficiency reigns at Philippe's, where patrons place and pay for their orders at a long deli counter. Seating is plentiful, and one can dine at long communal tables or seek out wooden booths. With sawdust-strewn floors, the restaurant retains much of the character of its earlier years.

Sandwich

While most people associate the French Dip Sandwich with roast beef, today's specialty at Philippe the Original can be ordered with roast beef, roast pork, leg of lamb, ham, or roast turkey, all served on a French roll that has been dipped in natural gravy resulting from roasting the meat. Sandwiches at Philippe's can be ordered single, double, triple, or quadruple dipped, and the restaurant makes its own special hot mustard.

The following recipe is based on the roasting method for beef supplied by Pat Bruno for his Chicago Italian Beef sandwiches, which were derived, according to legend, from the French Dip sandwich. For beef stock, see Chuck Taggart's recipe for Creole Roast Beef for Po-Boys.

The French Dip

1 4-pound sirloin tip beef roast,
trimmed of excess fat
Ground black pepper
1 cup homemade beef stock
1½ cups cold homemade beef stock
1 teaspoon liquid garlic
5 – 6 French bread rolls or 6-inch lengths
of French bread

Preheat oven to 475°. Sprinkle roast all over with plenty of ground black pepper, pressing it into the meat as much as possible. Place meat in a small roasting pan, and add the 1 cup of beef stock. Roast the beef at 475° for 35 minutes, then reduce the oven temperature to 400 ° and roast for 40 minutes. Do not turn off the oven.

Remove roast from oven and pour the 1½ cups cold beef stock into the bottom of the roasting pan. Let stand 15 – 20 minutes. Add garlic juice to broth in bottom of pan, and return the roast to the oven. Roast until meat reaches the desired degree of doneness for rare or medium, testing with a meat thermometer. (Some people like their beef for French dip well done and falling into pieces while others prefer medium rare to medium beef.)

Remove pan from oven, and set roast on a platter or caving board to cool slightly before carving. Transfer the au jus to a small, wide pan and keep it warm over low heat.

Cut rolls or bread open horizontally and, if desired, remove some of the bread from the inside, creating a pocket to hold the beef. Slice beef as thinly as possible. Dip rolls quickly into the au jus, generously fill with sliced beef, and serve immediately. Yield: 5 – 6 sandwiches.

Note: Garlic juice is available in liquid form or spray bottles from gourmet food shops. If using garlic spray, note that eight spritzes are equal to 1 teaspoon liquid garlic or one clove of garlic.

Where to Go:

Philippe the Original
1001 North Alameda Street
Los Angeles, CA

Chicago Italian Beef

Our search for the origin of the Italian beef sandwich led directly to Pasquale "Pat" Bruno, dining critic for the **Chicago Sun-Times**, cookbook author, and an expert on foods of the Windy City.

During the 1890s, Italian immigrants poured into Chicago's Near West Side, bordered by Polk and Taylor Streets, and by the 1920s, Italians made up the area's largest ethnic group. While stories and claims abound as to who should be rightfully credited for Italian beef, Bruno cuts straight to the chase, stating that it's clearly a descendant of the French Dip Sandwich that dates back to 1918 in Los Angeles (see French Dip Sandwich). He points out that expensive cuts of beef were definitely not a staple of Italian kitchens during the Depression years or even before, and it remained rare, in most Italian households, right through the 1950s, thus pretty much discrediting earlier claims to the origin of the sandwich.

Bruno is inclined to believe one legend, which says an Italian cook named Tony, who worked in a Greek coffee shop around 1948 or 1949, created the sandwich. Thinking the French dip served in that establishment was pretty bland, Tony threw in some garlic and herbs, a move that earned him accolades from just about everyone but the owner who fired him on the spot. Undaunted, Tony opened a successful Italian beef stand down the street and the rest is history.

Sandwich

Italian beef sandwiches are a Chicago favorite, and ex-patriots from the area have been known to use any excuse to get back home for a quick fix. The basis of the sandwich is very thinly sliced roast beef that has been seasoned with Italian herbs and spices. The beef slices are dipped in the thin, Italian-style "gravy" (actually an au jus created from the roasting process), highly flavored with garlic, ground black pepper, crushed red pepper, basil, and oregano. The beef is then placed onto a crusty roll (that may or may not also be dipped in the gravy), and topped with giardiniera, an Italian relish composed of finely chopped vegetables like hot peppers, celery, carrots, and spices in olive oil. More sweet or hot peppers may top it off. A "combo" sandwich calls for the addition of a grilled Italian sausage.

Because many beef stands offer only counter eating, fans have developed the famous "Chicago lean," described by Pat Bruno as follows: "feet spread about as wide as your shoulders, elbows on the counter, lean forward as you bite."

From his book *Chicago's Food Favorites: A Guide to More Than 450 Favorite Eating Spots* (now out of print), Pat Bruno also shares instructions on just how to order an Italian beef sandwich:

"Beef. Dry, sweet." Beef sandwich with a little less gravy and sweet peppers.
"Beef. Wet, hot." Beef sandwich with a lot of gravy (the roll is soaked with gravy before the beef is loaded into the roll) and hot peppers.
"Beef. Dry, hot." The same as the first one only with hot peppers instead of sweet.
"Combo." Half beef and half Italian sausage.

Pat Bruno's Italian Beef
Reprinted with permission from Pasquale "Pat" Bruno, Jr., dining critic for the *Chicago Sun-Times* and author of *The Great Chicago-Style Pizza Cookbook* and *Pasta Tecnica*.

Spice rub:
1 teaspoon dried basil
1 teaspoon dried oregano
1 teaspoon garlic powder
1 teaspoon ground black pepper
1 teaspoon salt
1 teaspoon red pepper flakes

1 4-pound sirloin tip beef roast, trimmed of excess fat
1 cup water
1½ cups cold water
2 – 3 teaspoons garlic juice or to taste (optional)
8 - 10 6-inch French or Italian bread rolls

Giardiniera (Italian hot pepper relish)
Chopped green bell peppers, grilled in olive oil

Preheat oven to 475°. Make a spice rub by combining the basil, oregano, garlic powder, ground black pepper, salt, and red pepper flakes.

Rub half of the spice rub over and around the beef roast. Press the mixture into the meat as much as possible. Place the meat in a roasting pan and add the one cup of water to the bottom of the pan; add more if necessary to cover bottom of pan. Roast the beef at 475° for 35 minutes. Reduce the temperature to 400° and roast for 40 minutes. Do not turn off the oven.

Remove beef from oven and pour $1^1/2$ cups remaining cold water into the bottom of the pan. Let stand 15 – 20 minutes. Add remaining seasoning mixture and garlic juice (optional) to the pan juices and water. Return meat to the oven and roast until a meat thermometer registers 160°, about 50 minutes. Note that because oven temperatures vary, the use of a meat thermometer is important.

Remove pan from oven and allow meat to stand and cool somewhat before slicing. Slice beef almost paper-thin; the right thinness is critical to ensure a good chew but without being too tough.

Transfer the juices to a saucepan and keep warm over low heat. Immerse the sliced beef into the warm gravy.

To serve, scoop about one-quarter to one-third pound of the beef out of the gravy with a fork. Load it into a French or Italian bread roll. Garnish with hot pepper giardiniera or grilled green bell peppers. Yield: 8 - 10 sandwiches.

Pat's Tips:

One of the "secrets" used by Chicago Italian beef stands is the addition of garlic juice to the pan juices during the final roasting. Garlic juice is available in liquid form or spray bottles from gour-met food shops. It does add immensely to the flavor. If using garlic spray, note that eight spritzes are equal to 1 teaspoon liquid garlic or one clove of garlic.

It is not the custom of Italian beef stands to undercook the beef. In fact, more often than not, the beef is roasted until it is what you might call "medium well," which means very little red is visible.

If you like a "wet" beef sandwich, dip the roll into the gravy a bit before loading in the sliced beef.

Pat Bruno's Chicago-Style Giardiniera
Reprinted with permission from Pasquale "Pat" Bruno, Chicago food expert and dedicated fan of the Italian Beef Sandwich.

¼ **cup finely diced carrots**
¼ **cup sliced (1/8-inch thick) on the bias sport peppers**
¼ **cup very small cauliflower florets**
¾ **cup sliced (1/8-inch slices) on the bias celery**
¼ **to ½ cup sliced jalapeños, as desired, for mild or hot flavor**
1 **teaspoon dried oregano, crumbled**
½ **teaspoon finely chopped garlic**
⅔ **cup olive oil**
2 **tablespoons white wine vinegar**

In a non-reactive bowl or container, combine all the vegetables with the oregano and garlic. Add the oil and vinegar, and toss to combine. Cover and store in a cool place, but do not refrigerate. Giardiniera should be made at least one day ahead of use in order to allow flavors to infuse. Serve as a topping for Italian beef sandwiches. The amount used on each sandwich varies according to taste, but approximately 3 generous tablespoons per sandwich works just fine. Yield: 2 $^1/2$ cups.

Notes: Sport peppers are a Chicago favorite, and they are served on everything from classic Chicago hot dogs to Italian beef sandwiches. Once known as the "Mississippi Sport Pepper," sport peppers belong to the serrano chile family, and most of them are now imported from Mexico. Look for sport peppers, sold in jars, in the condiment section of the supermarket.

Crushed red pepper flakes may be substituted for the jalapeños. If desired, vegetable oil may substituted for olive oil.

Where to Go:

The following locations are all in Chicago:

Mr. Beef
666 N. Orleans Street

Al's # 1 Italian Beef
1079 W. Taylor Street

Buona Beef
6745 W. Roosevelt Road
Berwyn, IL plus 8 other locations

Need a Quick Fix?
Giardiniera and sport peppers can be ordered from:

Vincent Formusa Company
710 W. Grand Avenue
Chicago, IL 60610
Telephone: (312) 421-0485

Hot giardiniera can be ordered from:

The Vermont Country Store
http://www.vermontcountrystore.com

Beef on Weck

Much of the German immigration to America began in the 1820s, swelling to larger numbers in the 1840s, with most of the new arrivals entering through the port of New York City. Although many remained in that area, others, traveling by rail, made their way to Buffalo, New York, where a large population boasting German heritage still exists today.

According to Richard Pillsbury in **No Foreign Food: The American Diet in Time and Place**, German immigrants had a major influence on American cuisine, and perhaps their foremost contribution was in the introduction of lager beer and new brewing techniques around the 1840s. Nowhere was this more evident than in Buffalo, a city, it is said, that was conceived in a tavern by men imbibing alcoholic beverages. German immigrants settled in Buffalo's East Side, and they were instrumental in building a thriving brewery business that has been well documented by Steve Powell, director of a comprehensive history site at http://www.buffalonian.com. By 1872, Buffalo had more than 35 breweries, and those breweries owned most of the taverns in a city that once boasted a bar on nearly every corner. In 1908, consolidation had reduced the number of breweries to 25, but statistics record the fact that if all the beer they produced in that year replaced water flowing over Niagara Falls, it would have taken a minute and eighteen seconds to clear the brink. Saloons had become the center of social and political activity for the workingman, and many visited their local tavern two or three times a day.

In the heyday of saloons and taverns, which ran from the 1880s right up to Prohibition, Bruce Aidells and Denis Kelly, authors of **Real Beer and Good Eats**, note that proprietors offered a free lunch to their patrons. Sometimes, the lunch cost a nickel or a dime, but it was still a good deal. Buffet tables were loaded with hearty foods like ham, roast beef, pickled herring and pig's feet, and sardines, all accompanied by raw onions, hot mustard, and rye bread. Saloon owners made sure that the food was plenty salty so that patrons would work up a thirst and wash it all down with more beer, a tactic that was obviously good for business.

It was during this period that Buffalo's famous "Beef on Kümmelweck" sandwich was born. Although documentation on the exact origin of the sandwich disappeared over time, legend has it that the kümmelweck roll was brought from the Black Forest by a German baker named William Wahr. Kümmel, the German word for caraway, was sprinkled over the top of Kaiser rolls along with large grains of coarse pretzel salt, and the rolls were sold to the saloons. It wasn't long before roast beef was piled into the rolls, a good dollop of feisty hot horseradish was added, and "Beef on weck," as it's called by the locals, was the result.

Schwabl's, in the Buffalo suburb of West Seneca, was established in 1837, and it may be the oldest continuously operating restaurant in New York State. Known for their beef on weck sandwiches, Schwabl's also offers homemade German potato salad and birch beer on draught.

Buffalonians and visitors alike often make a stop at Charlie the Butcher's Kitchen, near the airport, to stock up on beef on weck sandwiches. While some folks eat their fill prior to departure, others take a load home for those former Buffalonians pining for the famous sandwich in distant parts of the country.

Sandwich

Beef on weck sandwiches are based on the kümmelweck roll, apparently produced only in the Western New York (Buffalo and Rochester) area. The roll is the perfect conveyance for thinly sliced roast beef carved from thirty- and forty-pound roasts typically prepared by Buffalo area taverns. The bottom of the roll is piled high with thinly carved roast beef, the top of the roll is dipped into au jus, and the sandwich is served to diners who, more likely than not, will add Buffalo's condiment of choice, freshly grated, spicy-hot horseradish guaranteed to clear the sinuses.

Charlie the Butcher's Beef on Weck
Restaurants specializing in beef on weck typically prepare 30 to 40 pound beef roasts, but Buffalo's Charlie the Butcher shares the following version, suitable for home preparation.

4 kümmelweck rolls (see recipe below)
20 ounces thinly sliced, cooked, quality grade roast beef, purchased from the deli counter
1 cup au jus, also available from the deli counter, heated
Horseradish (optional)

Cut rolls in half. Dip each 5-ounce serving of beef briefly into the warm au jus and place on bottom of roll. Dip the top of each roll into warm au jus, and place over roast beef. For an authentic taste sensation, pass the horseradish, which should be spread lavishly atop the beef. Serve immediately. Yield: 4 sandwiches.

Charlie the Butcher's Kümmelweck Rolls

Beef on weck starts with a kümmelweck roll, made only in Western New York State. Thanks to Charlie the Butcher, who developed the recipe below, you can now make the requisite roll no matter where you live.

2 ounces coarse salt
2 ounces whole caraway seed
2 tablespoons warm water
1 teaspoon cornstarch
1/4 cup boiling water
12 fresh Kaiser or hard rolls

In a small bowl, combine coarse salt and caraway seed and set aside or store in a clean dry jar. In a small saucepan, dissolve cornstarch in warm water. Stir in the boiling water. Bring to a boil, and cook until mixture thickens enough to coat a spoon. Cool and store, covered, in the refrigerator if not using right away.

Preheat oven to 350°. Place Kaiser or hard rolls on a baking sheet. Brush tops of rolls with cornstarch mixture. Sprinkle each roll with an equal amount of caraway seed and salt mixture. Place rolls in the oven for about 4 minutes or just long enough for the caraway to dry. Remove from oven and use immediately to make beef on weck. Yield: 12 rolls.

Where to Go:

Loosemeat Sandwiches & The Sloppy Joe

During the latter part of the nineteenth century, ground beef became popular in America because it was economical as well as nourishing. Often, fillers like ketchup, mustard, breadcrumbs, onions, and peppers were added to stretch the meat even further. According to food historian Sandra Oliver, recipes for sloppy Joe-like concoctions began to appear as early as 1902 when Sarah Tyson Rorer included a recipe in **Mrs. Rorer's New Cook Book**.

Some food experts claim that the all-American sloppy Joe can be traced back to that quintessential midwestern favorite known as the loosemeat sandwich. Food sleuths Jane and Michael Stern uncovered the claim that David Heglin created the sandwich in 1924. He called it the "tavern" and served it at his restaurant, Ye Old Tavern, in Sioux City, Iowa. However, the Maid-Rite restaurants have a counter claim. They say Floyd Angell of Muscatine, Iowa, created it in 1926. Angell developed a special grind of meat and cooked it loosely rather than forming it into a hamburger patty, placed it on a roll, and the result was a new ground beef sandwich. Legend has it that Angell handed one of the sandwiches to a deliveryman who remarked that the sandwich was "made right." Angell went on to establish the Maid-Rite restaurant chain in 1927, a franchise operation that today boasts more than 80 outlets in Iowa and other Midwest states.

While the Maid-Rite loose-meat sandwich is still made in the original manner, somewhere along the way someone added ketchup, creating yet another sandwich called the sloppy Joe. Various restaurants have laid claim to the origin of the sloppy Joe. However, based on the number of eating establishments named "Sloppy Joe's" in the 1930s, it's likely that the sandwich was named after restaurants that served it.

The sloppy Joe was a favorite sandwich in the United States during World War II, especially because it offered a tasty way to stretch ground beef. While the sandwich was not mentioned by name, **Coupon Cookery** by Prudence Penny (a pseudonym used by food writers who wrote for the Hearst newspapers from the 1930s to the 1960s) lists hamburger as a recommended sandwich filling at a time when meat was rationed. Chopped meat sandwiches, moistened and flavored in a variety of ways including ketchup or chili sauce, were also featured in the 1944 edition of **Young America's Cook Book: A Cook Book for Boys and Girls Who Like Good Food**.

Both the loosemeat and sloppy Joe sandwiches increased in popularity during the late 1940s and 1950s, especially among working class families and teenagers who flocked to the new drive-in restaurants that featured them. Today, the sloppy Joe is known throughout the United States, whereas the loosemeat sandwich has retained its regional following. However, there is no argument about the fact that both sandwiches are a bit sloppy to eat. The Maid-Rite loosemeat sandwich is always served with a spoon so that diners can scoop up every savory bite. It gained nationwide renown when it was featured as the Lunch Box specialty of the house in a **Roseanne** episode called *Roseanne in the Hood*.

At Taylor's Maid-Rite in Marshalltown, Iowa, they butcher their own meat, which is then cooked up in a 75-year-old "cooker" right up where all the customers can see what's going on and get a tantalizing whiff of the delicious aromas. With the meat piled into buns, Maid-Rite loosemeat sandwiches are served with mustard, pickle, and onion (no ketchup is permitted). The sandwiches always come wrapped, even if they are to be eaten in-house. Taylor's recommends one of their vanilla malt milkshakes as an appropriate accompaniment to the tasty sandwich.

Sandwiches

The sloppy Joe is typically composed of browned ground beef combined with chopped onion, green pepper, and celery, to which ketchup and sometimes tomato soup are added, cooked until thickened, and used to fill hamburger buns. Loosemeat sandwiches are simply twice-ground beef cooked and seasoned with a secret ingredient or two (depending upon the restaurant), piled into hamburger buns, and topped off with mustard, pickles and/or chopped onions. Sometimes ketchup is available, but it's generally frowned upon.

Iowa-Style Loosemeat Sandwiches

2½ pounds twice-ground beef
2 cups water
¼ cup dried onion flakes
1 teaspoon ground black pepper
1 tablespoon unseasoned instant meat tenderizer
2 tablespoons instant beef bouillon granules
1 14½-ounce can beef or chicken broth

8 hamburger buns, toasted if desired
Chopped fresh onion
Mustard
Pickles

In a medium-sized cooking pot, combine ground beef with water and simmer over medium heat until beef is cooked. In a large colander, drain water from beef and return beef to the cooking pot. Add remaining ingredients and simmer over medium heat until liquid is almost completely evaporated, about 30 minutes. Spoon beef into the buns and serve immediately with condiments. Be sure to give everyone a spoon so they can scoop up any stray beef that escapes the buns! Yield: 8 sandwiches.

Where to Go:

Sloppy Joes are found throughout the United States, typically at diners, delis, and luncheonettes like this one in New Jersey:

Town Hall Delicatessen
18 South Orange Avenue
South Orange, NJ

The loosemeat sandwich is the flagship product of the Maid-Rite restaurant chain in Iowa and other Midwestern states. It's also featured at several independent restaurants.

Taylor's Maid-Rite
106 South Third Avenue
Marshalltown, IA

Need a Quick Fix?

Taylor's Maid-Rite ships plain, frozen Maid-Rites door-to-door. Pickles and onions come too, in separate containers. You can order by phone or via their web site.

Taylor's Maid-Rite
106 South Third Avenue
Marshalltown, IA 50158
Web site: http://www.maidrite.com
Telephone: 1-641-753-9684

The Reuben & The Rachel

The origin of the Reuben sandwich, composed of corned beef, Swiss cheese, and sauerkraut, is a hotly contested issue involving at least three separate camps. The first story is based in New York City, where it's claimed that Arnold Reuben, a German immigrant, created it in 1914. Because she was so hungry, actress Annette Seelos asked for a big combo sandwich when she came into Reuben's Restaurant after her nightly performance, and the Reuben was the result. However, that sandwich was composed of rye bread, baked Virginia ham, roast turkey, Swiss cheese, coleslaw, and Reuben's special Russian dressing, and it was called the "Reuben Special." Reuben's son, Arnold, Jr., said that years later, in the 1930s, a chef at the family restaurant, named Alfred Schueing, layered corned beef onto toasted dark pumpernickel bread and added cheese and sauerkraut, all the basic components of the sandwich that we know today as the Reuben.

An opposing claim comes from Omaha, Nebraska, where it's said that Reuben Kulakofsky, a grocer and owner of the Central Market, created a sandwich of corned beef, Swiss cheese, and sauerkraut on rye bread in the early 1920s for hungry, late-night poker players at the Blackstone Hotel. The sandwich was so well received that Charles Schimmel, owner of the hotel, put it on the menu and named it the Reuben in honor of its creator. In 1956, Fern Snider, a former waitress at the Blackstone, won a national sandwich competition with the recipe for the Reuben.

And then there is a third claim that the Reuben originated at the Cornhusker Hotel in Lincoln, Nebraska, in 1937. Supporting this theory is a menu from that same year listing the Reuben with its traditional ingredients. As of this writing, menus substantiating the other two claims have not yet publicly surfaced.

Somewhere along the line, the Rachel sandwich made its debut, most likely as a simple variation of the Reuben. Interesting is the fact that no individual or restaurant seems to have claimed it as their own.

Reuben Sandwich

Corned beef, usually made from beef brisket, is beef that has been "corned" or cured in salt. Pastrami is also made from beef that has been cured in salt brine, but it involves a second step whereby the meat is smoked over hardwood sawdust.

Today, the Reuben sandwich is usually composed of thinly sliced corned beef, Swiss cheese, sauerkraut, and Russian dressing piled between slices of rye bread and quickly grilled, resulting in a sandwich that is hot on the outside and cool within. Some recipes call for Thousand Island dressing instead of Russian dressing, and various restaurants often create their own versions of the traditional sandwich. A side of coleslaw traditionally accompanies the Reuben.

Rachel Sandwich

A variation on the Reuben, the Rachel sandwich can be made in a couple of different ways. First, there's the version whereby corned beef is substituted with thinly sliced turkey; in all other respects, this Rachel is the same as the Reuben. Then there's the version that calls for pastrami, Swiss cheese, coleslaw, and Russian dressing on rye. Finally, the Rachel sometimes shows up made with rye bread, pastrami, thinly sliced onion, thinly sliced tomato, and Swiss cheese, and it's then grilled.

The Rachel

2 slices rye bread
¼ pound thinly sliced pastrami
1 or 2 thin slices of Swiss cheese
1 thin slice of tomato
1 thin slice of onion
Kosher dill or half sour pickles (optional)

Butter one side of each slice of bread. Place the first slice, buttered side down, in a medium frying pan. Pile on the slices of pastrami and Swiss cheese. Cover with slices of tomato and onion and top with the other slice of bread, buttered side up. Cover and grill, over medium heat, until toasted on both sides and cheese is melted. Serve with kosher dills or half sours.
Yield: 1 sandwich.

Where to Go:

Need a Quick Fix?
When nothing else will do, New York's four most famous delis will ship their pastrami and corned beef. Carnegie will also ship sandwiches, and the mail order menu from Second Avenue Deli is staggering. Just call them to order.

Katz's Delicatessen: (212) 254-2246
Carnegie Delicatessen: (800) 334-5606
Stage Delicatessen: (212) 245-7850
Second Avenue Deli: (800) 692-3354
or 212-677-0606

There's nothing like a New York deli for traditional sandwiches made from hand carved corned beef and pastrami. Katz's Deli, founded in 1888, is the oldest and largest. The movie *When Harry Met Sally* was filmed there, and Katz's is also known for its creation of the famous World War II advertising slogan, "Send a salami to your boy in the army." The sign still hangs in the restaurant. Katz's is located in Manhattan's Lower East Side, the historic neighborhood where many immigrant Jews first lived after arriving in America. Once home to pushcart peddlers, the area is a terrific source of traditional Jewish foods like bagels, bialys, and excellent deli meats. The Second Avenue Deli, founded in Manhattan's Lower East Side in 1954, is kosher and a favorite neighborhood eating spot still relatively unknown among tourists. Two other famous delicatessens, Carnegie and Stage, are located in Midtown Manhattan, and they offer table as well as counter service. All four delis are known for the great sour and half-sour pickles that accompany their sandwiches and for the "ambiance" provided by brusque countermen who fill orders at top speed and who expect patrons to quickly belt out their orders.

All of the following delis are located in New York City:

Katz's Delicatessen
205 E. Houston Street

Carnegie Delicatessen
854 Seventh Avenue

Stage Delicatessen
834 Seventh Avenue

Second Avenue Deli
156 Second Avenue

The Pastrami Dip

The pastrami dip sandwich was created sometime in the 1940s or 1950s by hot dog stands in the Los Angeles, California, area. Looking for a way to keep pastrami from drying out, they borrowed from the French Dip Sandwiches served at Philippe the Original and dipped their pastrami into au jus. The pastrami dip is actually a "double dip," since both the pastrami and the French roll in which it's served are dipped into the "gravy."

The Hat, whose original location in Alhambra, California, was established in 1951, is known as a mecca for pastrami and most especially for its pastrami dip sandwiches that include mustard and dill pickles. Junior's, the well-known Jewish deli in West Los Angeles, also serves the pastrami dip sandwich.

Where to Go:

The Hat
1 West Valley Road
Alhambra, CA

Junior's
2379 Westwood Boulevard
West Los Angeles, CA

St. Louis Brain Sandwich

At one time, St. Louis, Missouri, was home to a huge meat packing business and, of course, the slaughterhouses that go along with an industry that reached its peak there in the 1950s and 1960s. Beef and pork brains were not big sellers, and they were typically discarded. St. Louis taverns seized the opportunity to offer an economic item, for both the establishment and the patron, on their menus, and the brain sandwich became a popular item with locals.

While the sandwich still has a following, writer Pamela Lowney says it's mostly senior citizens, fans of the sandwich during its heyday, who provide the largest consumer group for this delicacy that's beginning to fade from the food scene. Perhaps that's because diners today demand increased taste and punch in their food, and those familiar with brain sandwiches flatly state that there isn't much flavor in the meat itself. Actually, most of the taste comes from the accompanying onion and condiments. Nevertheless, the folks at Ferguson's Pub claim

Real Deli-Style Pickles

No self-respecting Jewish-style deli would forego serving really great pickles. Half-sours are also known as "half-done" pickles, and they taste like a crunchy, garlicky cucumber. And then there are the half-sour tomatoes, green tomatoes that are soaked in pickling brine. If you can't get to the legendary Gus's Pickles in New York City's Lower East Side, help is now available. The enterprising owners of Pickle-Licious teamed up with Gus's, and they'll ship both half-sour pickles and tomatoes.

Pickle-Licious
Telephone: (201) 302-9139
Fax: (201) 302-9363
Web site: http://www.picklelicious.com

they sell thirty to forty brain sandwiches a week - not bad for a sandwich that faces tough competition from all those St. Louis barbecue joints!

Sandwich

The brain sandwich consists of breaded brains deep-fried for 25 to 30 minutes, since the meat must be well done. When cooked, the brains resemble small brown pillows. Custom dictates that brains be served on rye or plain old white bread along with pickles, onion, and a choice of horseradish or mustard. A side of potato chips or coleslaw is customarily included.

Because the preparation of brains involves significant cleaning by knowledgeable processors, the number of restaurants offering the delicacy in St. Louis has dwindled considerably. Dieckmeyer's, a long time St. Louis establishment once known for its brain sandwich, has closed its doors, and customers now flock to one of two taverns, the Back Door and Ferguson's Pub, that still cater to devotees.

Where to Go:

Ferguson's Pub
2925 Mt. Pleasant
St. Louis, MO

Back Door
9538 Gravois
St. Louis, MO

Chicken Fried Steak Sandwich

If Texas has a "national dish," it has got to be chicken fried steak. Of course, it's found throughout the Southwest, and so ubiquitous is it on the menus of roadside eateries that some veteran travelers, like Donald "Dutch" Martinich, refer to Route 66, which traverses Texas from Shamrock to Glenrio, as "The Chicken Fried Steak Highway." The dish is so popular in Houston that it has sometimes been jokingly referred to as "Houston Fried Steak." Texans and Houstonians, both, are so devoted to it that it's even served up in the form of a sandwich. We quote the following, which conveys Texas' reverence for chicken fried steak:

"As splendid and noble as barbecue and Tex-Mex are, both pale before that Great God of Beef dish, chicken-fried steak. No single food better defines the Texas character; it has, in fact, become a kind of nutritive metaphor for the romanticized, prairie-hardened personality of Texans. Chicken-fried steak is the toughest piece of beef, tenderized and civilized and brought to the table as the nucleus of a royal feast, the hub of what nationally syndicated columnist Liz Smith (a Texan) called "a 5,000-calories meal."

– Jerry Flemmons, **Plowboys, Cowboys and Slanted Pigs**, TCU Press. Reprinted with permission from Texas Christian University Press.

Texas cuisine has solid roots in Southern cooking, so it's not surprising that food historian Sandra Oliver referred back to nineteenth century Southern cookbooks in her search for the origin of chicken fried steak. It turns out that dredging steaks in flour before frying, and then covering them with gravy, is an old practice. In **The Virginia House-wife**, published in 1824, Mary

Randolph provides a recipe for "A Fricado of Beef" that follows just such a method. Fifty-five years later, in 1879, Marion Cabell Tyree gave two more recipes in **Housekeeping in Old Virginia**. "Beefsteak Fried with Onions" calls for dredging the meat in flour, frying it in lard, and then making gravy with onions and the drippings. Her recipe for "Fried Steak" advocates beating Porterhouse or tenderloin steaks until "ragged," dredging them in flour, frying them, and then covering the steak with hot gravy. Old receipts for "country-fried steak," in a manner similar to today's chicken fried steak, were thus common, and the method of preparation was so ingrained that similar recipes are still used, sometimes with less tender cuts of beef.

In Texas, it's believed that early settlers and chuck wagon cooks brought these methods of preparing beef with them. Undoubtedly, German immigrants who came to Texas as early as 1831, especially in the hill country around Austin and New Braunfels, brought recipes that included the preparation of wiener schnitzel in a manner very similar to the preparation of chicken fried steak. Originally made with veal, the early German settlers probably substituted less costly beef.

So where did chicken fried steak originate? Most likely, its basic preparation came with settlers from both the Southern United States and Germany, albeit in slightly different form. Like most recipes, it was assimilated and adapted into the developing regional food culture, eventually emerging as the chicken fried steak known in Texas today. Some food historians date the introduction to the Depression years, when both the times and meat were tough. From every indication, however, the dish is much older than that, by about a hundred years.

Texas writer Robb Walsh basically agrees with this premise. Walsh also points out that the story in the **Lone Star Book of Records**, which credits the 1911 invention of chicken fried steak to Jimmy Don Perkins, a café cook who mistook a customer's order, is false. But he does point out that Carol B. Sowa noted, in the **Best Read Guide to San Antonio**, that chicken fried steak had been incorporated into sandwiches that were served at Pig Stand Drive-Ins throughout the San Antonio area in the 1940s. This would certainly indicate that the popularity of the sandwich had been firmly established for several years, and that it commanded a loyal clientele.

The Texas Restaurant Association reports that CFS, the acronym for chicken fried steak, is served by 90% of its 4,000 members, and one official calculated that Texans order 800,000 steaks a day, not counting what is consumed at home. In Texas, chicken fried steak in the form of a sandwich or by itself, is served for breakfast, lunch, and dinner, always accompanied by cream gravy.

Sandwich

The chicken fried steak sandwich is typically composed of a beefsteak, usually round steak about a half inch thick, trimmed of fat and gristle, and tenderized. It's floured, dipped in an egg-milk batter, floured again, and plunged into deep fat (shortening or lard) until it's golden brown. It's served on a bun, sometimes toasted, or on Texas toast (usually white bread sliced twice as thick as normal and toasted), with a choice of condiments, including the traditional white milk or cream gravy that accompanies a chicken fried steak dinner. Other condiments of choice are cheese, mayonnaise, onion, and ketchup. Folks sometimes order the cream gravy on the side for dipping. French fries or potato chips normally accompany the sandwich.

Austin, Texas, Chef David Bulla is on a mission to restore what he sees as the former glory and dignity of the CFS. According to Bulla, a really great CFS shouldn't be delivered up in the deep-fried form that is so often found today. He advocates a return to frying the CFS in a cast iron skillet, and he also suggests using those better cuts of beef advocated so long ago by Marion Cabell Tyree in **Housekeeping in Old Virginia**.

Texas-Style Pan Fried Sirloin

Reprinted with permission from an article by Austin, Texas, Chef David Bulla entitled *Chicken Fried Steak – A Texas Tradition Revisited* on Texas Cooking Online at http://www.texascooking.com

1 teaspoon salt
1 teaspoon freshly ground black pepper
1 teaspoon granulated garlic
1 teaspoon good quality chili powder (optional)
2 top sirloin steaks about ¼ inch thick and as big as you like them
1 cup buttermilk
1 egg
1 cup all-purpose flour
1 cup fresh bread crumbs
1 cup (more or less) vegetable oil

Mix together the salt, pepper, garlic, and chili powder. Liberally season the steaks on both sides. With the coarse spike side of a meat tenderizing hammer, pound the seasoned steaks to tenderize them and work the seasoning into the meat. Be careful not to pound the steaks too thin, but you have to use enough force to actually start breaking down the meat fibers a little bit. Just putting a nice hammer mark on the steak won't do much. You want to make the steak a little thinner and a little larger to accomplish the tenderizing process.

In a bowl, mix the buttermilk with the egg. Set up your breading station with a bowl of flour, the bowl containing the buttermilk-egg mixture, and a bowl of breadcrumbs. Dredge the steak in the flour, coating it evenly. Shake off the excess flour, and dredge the steak in the buttermilk-egg mixture. Now dredge the steak in the breadcrumbs. Make sure the steaks are evenly coated. Set steaks aside on a plate; you can layer them between sheets of waxed paper.

In a cast iron skillet, heat the oil over medium heat. You want to have enough oil in the pan to come a little more than half way up the side of the steaks when they are cooking. You do not want to submerge the steaks in oil. The temperature should be around 300°. It will vary during the cooking process, but you want to maintain a temperature above 250° and no more than about 350°. Adjust the heat as necessary while you cook. You will know if your pan is too hot if your steak starts to get too dark. You want a nice simmer happening in the pan.

When the oil is hot, add your steaks. If your skillet is too small, you can cook in batches. When you start to see the juices bleeding through the top crust of the steak, it's time to turn it. Fry about 5 minutes per side. You are looking for a nice brown color on the crust, like the color of dark wood, but not the color of chocolate. You should turn your steaks only once. When both sides are done, remove them from the pan and drain on a brown paper bag or paper towels. Keep steaks in a warm oven until the gravy is ready to go. Yield: 2 steaks or enough for 4 CFS sandwiches.

Note: Choose steaks that have a good marbling of fat but that are trimmed of large fatty areas.

Creamy Pan Gravy
Reprinted with permission from an article by Austin, Texas, Chef David Bulla entitled *Chicken Fried Steak – A Texas Tradition Revisited* on Texas Cooking Online at http://www.texascooking.com

There is a term in classic French cooking called "fond." This term describes the browned, caramelized, concentrated residue that remains in the pan after something has been cooked. The fond is what you are after when you "deglaze" a pan. It's what adds richness to any pan sauce. And fond is what's missing in most restaurant versions of cream gravy. This version is a little different in that it also has chicken stock and a little wine.

2 tablespoons reserved oil from pan
2 tablespoons all-purpose flour
¼ cup dry white wine
1 cup chicken stock
1 cup half-and-half
1 teaspoon coarsely ground fresh black pepper
1 teaspoon salt

From the pan you just fried your steaks in, drain off all the oil into a container. Measure out 2 tablespoons of the oil and return it to the cast iron frying pan. Turn the heat to medium-high. Add flour and cook for a few minutes, whisking, until a paste is formed and there are no lumps in the flour.

Add the wine and the chicken stock. Use a whisk to quickly incorporate the flour mixture into the liquid, ensuring there are no lumps. Bring the mixture up to a simmer. The gravy will get very thick at this point. Scrape the bottom of the pan with a wooden spoon to get all the fond incorporated into the gravy. Add the half-and-half a little at a time until the desired consistency is achieved. You want a thick sauce but not a paste. Season the gravy with salt and pepper, adjusting amounts to taste. Yield: enough gravy for 2 steaks or for dipping 4 CFS sandwiches.

Chicken Fried Steak Sandwich
Reprinted with permission from Austin, Texas, Chef David Bulla.

Texas-Style Pan Fried Sirloin, prepared in 4 equal pieces (recipe above)
Cream Pan Gravy (recipe above)
4 good quality hamburger buns or Kaiser rolls, toasted if desired
Condiments (optional):
Mayonnaise
Lettuce
Thinly sliced fresh tomato
Pickled jalapeño peppers
Cheddar cheese
Sliced avocado

On each bun, place a piece of chicken fried steak and garnish as desired. Serve immediately with small bowls of hot Creamy Pan Gravy for dipping. Yield: 4 sandwiches.

Chef Bulla's Notes: Cut your steak to the approximate size of the bread you would use. The most common bread would be a round, soft bread with a medium-firm crust, like a good quality hamburger bun or Kaiser roll. Don't use bread that is too crusty and that you have to work hard to bite through, because you'll end up with a mess when you try to bite through a chewy bun and a fairly chewy fried steak with a delicate crust. Similarly, if you use soft white sandwich bread, you wouldn't have enough support for the CFS, and the result would be a fairly messy experience. The way I happen to like my CFS sandwich is simple, with mayo, lettuce, and good fresh tomato. I also like having a small side of gravy in a bowl large enough to dip into – like a Texas French Dip. You can treat the CFS like a burger and top it with whatever you like. Good combinations are pickled jalapeño and cheddar cheese, or avocado with lettuce and tomato.

Where to Go:

Popular Houston locations for chicken fried steak sandwiches include Goodson's Café in Tomball (just outside Houston), which is known for serving the biggest "legal" CFS in the state.

Goodson's Café
27931 Tomball Parkway

Longhorn Café
509 Louisiana

59 Diner
8125 Katy Freeway

HAM & PORK: EVERYTHING BUT THE SQUEAL

It has been said that America was literally created on a diet of pork. As settlement expanded, hogs were easily transported, and required little special care relative to diet or general oversight. And pork, in its many guises where virtually nothing went to waste, was a staple in the diets of early Americans, providing a full range of cured products such as smoked ham, sausage, bacon, and salted and pickled pork, meats that could be easily stored for later use. The versatility of pork has ensured its continued popularity throughout the United States today, and it makes its appearance in many of our most popular sandwiches.

Cuban & Medianoche Sandwiches

It is generally agreed that the Cuban sandwich was brought to the United States by Cuban cigar workers who migrated to the Tampa, Florida, area around the turn of the twentieth century. Enterprising Cubans established cigar factories at Ybor City, a few miles east of Tampa, and it soon became known as "Little Havana."

Originally known as the "mixto" or mixed sandwich, the Cuban, as it's called today, became a workingman's lunch for those employed in the Tampa cigar industry with little time to eat. They were carried to work secured together by toothpicks, and they rapidly became a status symbol - after all, not everyone could afford to eat – and those who could, returned to work with a toothpick in their teeth.

According to food historian Andy Huse, those first Cuban immigrants in Ybor City were quite innovative when it came to recreating their favorite sandwich from back home. They often used tailor's irons to press and glaze the sugar coating into their hams, and they also used the irons to press and grill their sandwiches.

Authentic crusty Cuban bread is considered crucial to a good sandwich, and it, too, has a history. According to Steve Otto of the **Tampa Tribune**, Cuban bread got its long thin shape due to a flour shortage in Cuba at the time of the Revolution of 1875. It's baked with palmetto leaves inserted along the top of the formed loaf, creating the distinct split crust. Otto also reports that in the old days, Ybor City bakers provided home delivery, impaling the loaves of bread onto nails that customers hammered next to their front doors. In **The Florida Cookbook**, authors Jeanne Voltz and Caroline Stuart report that bakeries were among the first businesses established by Cubans fleeing their homeland in 1959 and 1960. Loaves of Cuban bread are traditionally made in 36-inch lengths and are thus sometimes called "yard bread."

A recent immigrant to the United States, the proprietor of Dona Rossina's in Tampa makes her own Cuban bread and uses mojo pork (pork marinated in mojo marinade) in her sandwiches, touches of true authenticity that draw many fans of the Cuban sandwich to the restaurant. Hugo's in Tampa is especially known for its Cuban sandwiches pressed in the traditional manner.

While most of the old cigar factories are now closed, Ybor City is a historical section of Tampa, and the area is a veritable bastion of great Cuban food. Although Tampa may claim title to the establishment of the Cuban sandwich cult in Florida, Miami is by no means left behind. There are dozens and dozens of great places to enjoy the sandwich there as well. The Cuban rules as the favorite sandwich among Floridians, with tens of thousands sold daily, and its popularity is spreading throughout the country.

Cuban Sandwich

Authentic Cuban sandwiches are based on crusty Cuban bread, similar to French bread but flatter and a bit more dry, and composed of thin slices of sugar cured ham (preferably imported from Spain), thinly sliced pork that has been bathed in mojo (a marinade of sour orange juice, oil, salt, oregano, garlic, and peppers) and slowly roasted, Swiss cheese, and thin slices of sour or dill pickle. Most diners request the optional mustard.

Additions like Genoa salami (contributed by Italian immigrants), mayonnaise, lettuce, tomato, and onion have become popular in the past forty years but are considered heresy by those who insist on authenticity and who follow the old way of just spreading on a bit of butter inside and out. In the old days, the sandwich was brushed on the outside with a small amount of pork drippings. Once assembled, the Cuban is placed in a sandwich press that compresses the sandwich while melting the cheese and heating the meats.

Medianoche Sandwich

The medianoche is the "sister sandwich" to the Cuban, and its name translates to "midnight" – apparently because it's eaten in the early hours of the morning after a night on the town. The difference between the two is in the bread: the medianoche is made on a smaller Cuban egg roll that is sweeter in taste, similar to challah.

In searching for the definitive Cuban sandwich recipe for home use, we discovered an excellent web site that serves as a guide to just about everything Cuban, including food. Billing themselves as Three Guys From Miami,™ Raúl Musibay, Glenn Lindgren, and Jorge Castillo host iCuban.com: The Internet Cuban,™ generously sharing their considerable knowledge that's spiced up with plenty of humor, travel recommendations, terrific recipes, and much more. They've even written a cookbook entitled **Cuban Food with Attitude** that's not to be missed by anyone interested in great Cuban cooking.

Cuban Sandwich
Recipe courtesy of Three Guys From Miami™
iCuban.com: The Internet Cuban™
http://icuban.com

Cuban bread (or substitute French bread if you must, but not a baguette)
Butter, softened
Sliced dill pickles
1 pound thinly sliced roasted Cuban pork

(recipe follows)
1 pound thinly sliced good quality ham
1/2 pound mild Swiss cheese, sliced
Yellow mustard (optional)
Mayonnaise (optional)
Vegetable cooking spray

Preheat a pancake griddle or a large frying pan. Cut the bread into four sections, each about 8 inches long. Slice these in half horizontally and spread butter on the inside of both halves. Generously layer sandwiches with filling ingredients in the following order: pickles, roasted pork, ham, and cheese. Spread with the optional mustard or mayonnaise if desired.

Lightly spray the hot griddle or frying pan with a little vegetable cooking oil, and add the first sandwich. (Make sure that your griddle or frying pan is not too hot or the crust will burn before the cheese melts.) Place a heavy iron skillet or bacon press on top of the sandwich to flatten it. (You really want to smash the sandwich, compressing the bread to about one-third of its original size.) Grill the sandwich for 2 – 3 minutes on each side, until the cheese is melted and the bread is golden. Repeat process for remaining sandwiches. Slice each sandwich in half diagonally and serve. Yield: 4 generous sandwiches.

Tips from Three Guys From Miami™:

Bring the meats and cheese to room temperature before making the sandwiches. This will avoid burning the bread and the cheese will melt perfectly. This is especially helpful when there is a lot of meat in the sandwiches.

Serrano ham, a dry, slightly salty ham similar to Italian prosciutto, is great for Cuban sandwiches and makes a very tasty addition.

For extra flavor, sprinkle a little mojo or meat juice on the pork and ham before adding the cheese.

Using mustard or mayonnaise is a personal choice. We find that the best Cuban sandwiches don't need either ingredient. The butter, natural meat juices, and yes, even the pickle juice, give it all the moistness and flavor it needs. At lunch counters, we've seen many people dipping their sandwich into a little mustard. So it's perfectly acceptable to serve these condiments on the side.

Roast Pork for Cuban Sandwiches
Recipe courtesy of Three Guys From Miami™
iCuban.com: The Internet Cuban™
http://icuban.com

Marinade:
3 cloves garlic
1 teaspoon salt
1 tablespoon dried oregano
1 cup minced onion
1 cup sour orange juice (or use substitute recommended in note below)
1/2 cup Spanish olive oil

1 2-pound boneless center-cut pork loin roast

Marinade: Mash the garlic and salt together with a mortar and pestle. (If you don't have a mortar and pestle, use a rolling pin and a cutting board.) Place the mixture in a small bowl. Add oregano, onion, and the sour orange to the mash and mix thoroughly. Heat oil in a small saucepan over medium heat, add the mash to the oil, and whisk the mixture together. Remove from heat and set the marinade aside.

Thoroughly pierce the pork roast with a sharp knife or fork. Set aside a small amount of the marinade for use during the roasting period. Pour remaining marinade over the pork, cover, and refrigerate for two to three hours.

Preheat oven to 325°. Remove pork from refrigerator and place it on a rack in a roasting pan. Sprinkle remaining marinade over pork. Roast until completely cooked and a meat thermometer registers 160°, about 20 minutes per pound. Baste occasionally with the pan juices. Remove pork from oven and let it set for at least 20 minutes before thinly slicing the meat.

Bring remaining pan juices to a boil, and simmer until the juice is reduced by half. Use this juice to sprinkle onto the meat in the sandwiches.

Note: If you can't get sour oranges in your area, try equal parts of orange and grapefruit juices, or two parts orange juice to one part lemon juice and one part lime juice.

Medianoche Sandwich
Recipe courtesy of Three Guys From Miami™
iCuban.com: The Internet Cuban™
http://icuban.com

For medianoche sandwiches, use all the same ingredients as listed for the Cuban sandwich, except substitute a medianoche bread loaf. The sweeter bread and smaller size are the only difference between a medianoche and a Cuban sandwich!

Need A Quick Fix?

Go to iCuban.com: The Internet Cuban™ for everything you could possibly need when it comes to Cuban recipes, fresh Cuban or Medianoche bread, Cuban sandwich presses, mojo marinades, and some 2,000 other Cuban specialty items. Orders are placed quickly via the Internet, and in no time at all, you'll be reproducing an authentic taste of Cuba right in your own home. Here's the web site: http://icuban.com

Where to Go:

In Miami, Florida, Three Guys From Miami™ recommend the Latin American Cafeteria. A local chain, it's basically a mom-and-pop-type operation with an atmosphere typical of Miami Cuban lunch counters. Skip the outdoor take-out window and go inside where you'll see Cuban sandwiches made to order, or sit at the counter and soak up the attention of the friendly waitresses. Here are some locations:

401 Biscayne Boulevard
2940 Coral Way
1750 W. 68 Street
97 SW 13th Street
9608 SW 72nd Street
2740 SW 27th Avenue
2940 NW 22nd Street
6820 Bird Road
9796 SW 24th Street

Tampa, Florida also has plenty of places to get great Cuban sandwiches:

La Ideal Grocery
2924 W. Tampa Bay Boulevard

Dona Rossina's
4816 Busch Boulevard East

Hugo's Spanish Restaurant
931 S. Howard Avenue

Snoots & Ears Sandwiches

Big bands and swing music have been around since the 1920s. One of the hot spots for band music during the late 1930s was the Club Reno in St. Louis. The establishment has been memorialized in various archive collections, and an interesting description published in the **Kansas City Star** includes mention of meal service from a horse-drawn lunch wagon stacked high with hog maws, liver, pig snoots and ears, chicken, fish, and pork. Patrons of the Club Reno would frequently buy a sandwich from the lunch wagon before grabbing a seat to enjoy the live musical entertainment. Sandwiches composed of pig snoots (aka snouts) or ears were popular, and today, they are still found in St. Louis, usually on soul food menus.

Sandwich

Pig snoots are typically baked, broken into small pieces, and then deep-fried until they are crisp and airy. Many liken them to pork rinds. Before being placed in the proverbial plain old white bread favored by St. Louis sandwich fans, the snoots are doused in barbecue sauce. At C&K BBQ in St. Louis, Daryle Brantley's delectable barbecue sauce is reminiscent of that found in some areas of South Carolina, and all sandwiches are served with potato salad actually in the sandwich itself.

Pig ears, on the other hand, are tenderized by hours of boiling and are served up, in all-too-disconcertingly recognizable shape, on white bread garnished with pickles and mustard.

Where to Go:

These popular eateries are all in the St. Louis, Missouri, area:

C&K BBQ (snoots and ears plus a host of BBQ specialties, especially rib tips)
4390 Jennings Station Road

Roper's Ribs (snoots)
6929 W. Florisant Avenue

Fat Matts
535 Matt Street

Spiedies

It's said that the spiedie, a sandwich made of meat cooked in a manner similar to shish kebab, was introduced to America by Augustine Iacovelli. In 1929, he immigrated to the Binghamton, New York, area from Civitella in Abruzzi, Italy. Ten years later, Iacovelli left his job at Endicott-Johnson, a shoe manufacturer, and struck out on his own, opening Augies restaurant in Endicott. There, he introduced the spiedie, solid working class food from his native Abruzzi, that became popular among foreign-born railroad workers and shoemakers.

The term spiedie comes from the Italian word "spiedo," meaning "spit" and/or "spiedini," meaning skewered meat. It's reported that Iacovelli's original spiedies, consisting of chunks of lamb, were impaled on wooden skewers and broiled over charcoal. Prior to cooking, and throughout the grilling process, the spiedies were sprayed with a sauce that Iacovelli called "Zuzu," consisting of wine vinegar, water, lemon juice, garlic, and mint. Cradled in a couple of slices of Italian bread, the spiedie was a satisfying meal for hungry workers.

Sandwich

Today, spiedies are still served throughout the Binghamton, New York, area. Indeed, the spiedie has attained a virtual cult status among locals, and so popular is the sandwich that it has spawned the annual Spiedie Fest held over a four-day period every August since 1983.

Meats used in the preparation of today's spiedies vary widely, running the gamut from lamb to chicken, beef, pork, and even wild game. And Iacovelli's sauce has evolved into a marinade, typically based on olive oil, garlic, and vinegar along with unique combinations of herbs favored in Italian cooking, such as mint, basil, oregano, parsley, and rosemary. The marinating process, which tenderizes the meat, can take up to a week but is never less than 24 hours. The spiedies are grilled and then plopped, minus the skewer, between slices of Italian bread or into buns with a judicious splash of extra marinade.

Bottled spiedie sauce, or marinade, can be found under many labels throughout the region, and expatriates nursing a craving for spiedies have their favorite brand shipped by the case to destinations throughout the United States. Curiously, the sandwich's popularity has not spread commercially beyond the Binghamton region.

Spiedies

Marinade:
1 cup vegetable oil
⅔ cup cider vinegar
2 tablespoons Worcestershire sauce
1 small onion, finely chopped
1 tablespoon finely chopped garlic
½ teaspoon salt
½ teaspoon sugar
½ teaspoon dried basil
½ teaspoon dried rosemary, crumbled
½ teaspoon dried marjoram

2½ pounds boneless lean pork or chicken, cut into 1-inch cubes (meat should have no fat, bone, or gristle)

8 hoagie rolls or hot dog buns
Butter or olive oil
Additional marinade (optional)

Marinade: In a 13 x 9-inch glass baking dish, combine all marinade ingredients and mix well to combine. Add cubed meat, tossing to coat it well. Cover and refrigerate for 24 hours, periodically turning the meat to coat it with marinade.

Heat grill and lightly rub cooking grid with vegetable oil to keep meat from sticking. Evenly divide meat cubes and thread them on six metal skewers. Discard marinade. Grill meat over medium heat until cooked and nicely browned on all sides, about 10 to 15 minutes.

Meanwhile, lightly butter rolls or brush them lightly with olive oil and place them under the broiler, or face-down on the grill, just until lightly browned. Remove meat from skewers, and place it directly into heated rolls. Yield: 6 sandwiches.

Note: If desired, make additional marinade to drizzle over the spiedies; do not re-use meat marinade. Spiedies can be a bit dry without the additional sauce.

Where to Go:

Sharkey's Restaurant
56 Glenwood Avenue
Binghamton, NY

Lupo's Spiedies
1001 North Street
Endicott, NY

Need a Quick Fix?

Folks born and bred in the Binghamton, New York, area but now living in other parts of the United States, order spiedie sauce from home. Those with major withdrawal symptoms also order the "Spiedie Survival Kit." You can, too. Check out the products at the Salamida Company web site, then phone or fax in your order.

Rob Salamida Company
71 Pratt Avenue
Johnson City, NY 13790
Telephone: (800) 545-5072
Fax: (607) 797-4721
Web site: http://www.spiedie.com

Pork Chop Sandwiches

As with so many of America's favorite sandwiches, the origin of the pork chop sandwich is contested. Perhaps it originated independently in various areas of the country. For starters, pork chop sandwiches are popular in America's pork producing states that include, in order of production size, Iowa, North Carolina, Minnesota, and Illinois. In the Midwest, a pork chop sandwich is ubiquitous at most any fair or festival, the equivalent of a hamburger elsewhere in the United States, and it is often called a "tenderloin sandwich."

Pork sandwiches enjoy a long epicurean history. The Browns feature instructions for a pork chop sandwich in their 1940 work **America Cooks: Favorite Recipes from the 48 States** in the section on Illinois subtitled "Chicago, Hog Butcher of the World." A boneless pork chop is broiled until brown and served on a bun spread with applesauce and a touch of chili sauce - not what we think of today when discussing a pork chop sandwich, but times change.

As popular as it may be in Illinois, however, it's in Iowa that the pork chop sandwich rules. Since World War II, Iowa has reigned as the foremost producer in what has been termed the "Swine Belt." Des Moines is also the home of the Iowa Pork Producers Association and the National Pork Board, industry associations that seek to promote pork through use of the slogan, "Pork – the other white meat®." To Iowa pig farmers, a "tenderloin" is the equivalent of chicken fried steak to Texas cattlemen.

Tracing the history of the pork tenderloin sandwich in Iowa is a bit of a challenge. Everyone knows about it, but it has been around so long that no one recalls how it got started. At Smitty's Tenderloin Shop in Des Moines, they proudly boast that they've been in the pork sandwich business since 1952. And with a tenderloin practically the size of a dinner plate, Smitty's claims it's the home of the "real whopper."

While nearly every sandwich shop in Iowa serves a tenderloin, a lot of folks have been sampling that served at the Northside Café in Winterset, a short hike southeast of Des Moines. The location is Madison County, recognizable as the place where *The Bridges of Madison County* was filmed. In the movie, Clint Eastwood is seen having lunch at the Northside. And then, of course, John Wayne was born in Winterset in 1907. With attractions like these, tour buses arrive almost daily, and visitors, hungry or just plain curious, head over to the café for an authentic Iowa tenderloin sandwich.

Although Montana is not known for its pork production, Pork Chop John's in Butte claims that its founder, John Burkland, is the inventor of the pork chop sandwich. Back in 1924, Burkland sold his Original Pork Chop Sandwich from the back of a wagon parked at the corner of Main and Mercury Streets. In 1932, riding the waves of success, Burkland opened a small lunch counter on Mercury Street where he continued to sell his popular sandwiches. The tiny shop, with only ten stools, is still open along with three other locations, an indication of the continued popularity of the pork chop sandwich in Montana.

It will come as no surprise to fans of *The Andy Griffith Show* that Snappy Lunch in Mt. Airy, North Carolina, is a veritable shrine for pork sandwiches. The hometown of actor Andy Griffith, Mt. Airy served as the model for the fictional Mayberry. In episode 9, entitled *Andy the Matchmaker*, Andy mentioned that he was on his way to the Snappy Lunch for a pork chop sandwich. According to the folks at Snappy Lunch, Griffith actually ate there as a student because the school didn't have a cafeteria in

those days. Guys checking out Snappy Lunch can also get a haircut at Floyd's City Barber Shop right next door. And every September, there's a festival called Mayberry Days.

Snappy Lunch first opened in 1923, and the current owner, Charles Dowell, bought a half interest in the business in 1951, buying the remainder of it in 1960. It was Dowell who introduced today's pork chop sandwich to Mt. Airy and Snappy Lunch patrons. An old Southern favorite, the original pork chop sandwiches were made from heavily breaded chops that still had the bone in them. Served on plain white bread, they were difficult to eat. Dowell introduced boneless chops and discovered a device called the "Tenderator," which he uses to tenderize them. The result is a pork chop the diameter of a salad plate that has put Snappy Lunch on America's sandwich map.

Sandwiches

A pork chop sandwich in the Midwest is a piece of boneless tenderloin pounded about a quarter of an inch thick, breaded, and then fried, deep fried, or sometimes grilled. Served on a toasted bun, condiments of choice for the tenderloin consist of mustard, pickle, and onion. New initiates are sometimes alarmed by the sight of the tenderloin, which hangs out from the bun, as it should, by at least an inch, and often much more, all the way around. At Smitty's Tenderloin Shop in Des Moines, Iowa, the bun pales in comparison to the twelve-inch diameter of the tenderloin.

The pork chop sandwich served at Pork Chop John's in Butte, Montana, no longer contains a whole pork chop; instead, it's made from lean ground pork that has been fashioned into a patty that's breaded and deep fried. It's typically served with mustard, onions, and pickle chips, but cheese, ketchup, and mayonnaise are available upon request.

At Snappy Lunch in Mt. Airy, North Carolina, they serve a tenderized, boneless pork chop lightly battered with a mixture of flour, milk, water, sugar, and salt, then deep-fried. The chop is placed in a roll and topped with sliced tomato, chopped onion, mustard, coleslaw, and Snappy's special meat chili.

Midwestern Pork Tenderloin Sandwich
Reprinted with permission from
the National Pork Board.

1 pound boneless pork loin or 1 pound boneless
center-cut pork chops
1 cup flour
1 teaspoon salt
1/2 teaspoon ground black pepper
Water
1/2 cup yellow cornmeal
Vegetable oil for frying
4 large sandwich buns, lightly toasted if desired

Condiments:
Mustard, Mayonnaise, Dill pickle chips
Ketchup, Sliced onion, Lettuce

Cut 4 one-inch thick slices of pork. Trim any exterior fat from edges. Put each slice of pork between pieces of plastic wrap. Using a wooden meat mallet or the side of a cleaver, pound vigorously until each slice is very thin and about 10 inches across. Mix flour with salt and ground black pepper.

Heat 1/2 -inch of oil in a deep, wide skillet to 365° F. Dip each slice of pork in water, then in flour mixture. Pat both sides with cornmeal. Fry tenderloins, one at a time, turning once, until golden brown on both sides, about 5 minutes total. Drain on paper towels and keep warm until all are cooked. Serve on buns with desired condiments. Yield: 4 sandwiches.

Where to Go:

Smitty's Tenderloin Shop
1401 S.W. Army Post Road
Des Moines, IA

Northside Café
61 W. Jefferson Street
Winterset, IA

Pork Chop John's
8 W. Mercury Street
Butte, MT

Snappy Lunch
125 N. Main Street
Mt. Airy, NC

Need a Quick Fix?
Smitty's Tenderloin Shop in Des Moines has been shipping frozen pork tenderloins to fans for years. Just give them a call.

Smitty's Tenderloin Shop
1401 S.W. Army Post Road
Des Moines, IA
515-287-4742

Although Pork Chop John won't send you an entire sandwich, you can order his famous pork chop patties and build your own. John's makes it easy: phone, fax, mail, or web orders are handled.

John's Sandwich Ship, Inc.
8 West Mercury Street
Butte, MT 59701-2098
Telephone: (406) 782-3159
Fax: (406) 782-6645
Web site: http://www.porkchopjohns.com

Taylor "Ham"

"Taylor Ham" is a major food group in the state of New Jersey. Actually, it's a pork roll that is now sold by several firms, but Taylor Provisions in Trenton, New Jersey, is said to have created the original product. Regardless of manufacturer, folks in Jersey insist upon calling it "Taylor Ham" even though the government seems to have stepped in at some point in time and said it was illegal to sell it as "ham." New Jersey expatriates scattered throughout the United States pine for it, and they unashamedly beg friends and relatives back home to ship a "fix" to them every so often.

Sandwich

It's no secret that folks in the New Jersey area continually seek out the best place for a fried "Taylor Ham" sandwich, whether for breakfast (usually with eggs) or lunch, when it's typically served on a hamburger bun or Kaiser roll with melted cheese.

New Jersey-Style Pork Roll (aka "Taylor Ham") Sandwich

2 tablespoons butter
4 thin slices pork roll ("Taylor Ham"), slit a couple of times around the edge to prevent curling
1 slice American cheese
1 hamburger bun or Kaiser roll, warmed

Melt butter in a medium frying pan. Add pork roll slices and fry over medium heat just until they begin to brown. Push the pork slices together a bit to bunch them up in the pan and lay the American cheese on top. Cover and cook a minute longer or until the cheese melts. Immediately place pork slices and cheese on the bun and serve. Yield: 1 sandwich.

Note: Fried onions make a tasty topping for this sandwich.

Where to Go:

Holly Moore, an authority on great sandwiches and creator of http://www.HollyEats.com, has been known to ferret out some of the best sandwich joints in the country. For "Taylor Ham" or pork roll sandwiches, Holly recommends Weber's Famous Root Beer, an old-fashioned drive-in restaurant located at Route 38 and King Road in Pennsauken, New Jersey. Here, Taylor pork roll is served on a soft hamburger bun with cheese, and patrons wash it down with a frosty mug of Weber's root beer. Carhops complete the ambiance.

• • • • • • • • • • • • • • • •

Need a Quick Fix?

There's now help for folks suffering from a craving for Taylor Pork Roll, aka "Taylor Ham." It can be purchased on the Internet and shipped fresh to your door. In addition to the Taylor (original) brand, two others are available: Kohler and Trenton.

Web site: http://www.porkrollxpress.com

Isaly's Chipped Chopped Ham

Pittsburgh is a city of legendary sandwiches, not least of which are those based on the Isaly's brand of Chipped Chopped Ham. Isaly's itself is a legend, and the source of fond memories throughout Western Pennsylvania and Ohio. Pittsburgher Brian Butko has written an in-depth history of the company in his book, **Klondikes, Chipped Ham & Skyscraper Cones: The Story of Isaly's.**

Isaly's traces its history back to 1833 when cheese maker Christian Isaly immigrated to Monroe County, Ohio, from Switzerland. Over the years, the Isaly family steadily expanded operations to include dairy farming and the establishment of a dairy company. Sometime around 1922, Isaly's introduced its famous Klondike Bar, made of vanilla ice cream dipped in chocolate and packaged in the now-familiar silver wrapper. Isaly's also became famous for its "Skyscraper Cones" filled high with six inches of ice cream. According to those in the know, favorite flavors were based on vanilla ice cream and included "White House" (incorporating whole maraschino cherries) and "Maricopa" (filled with butterscotch chunks). And then there was Isaly's "Chocolate Bubble" ice cream, featuring a mixture of whipped cream, chocolate syrup, and pecans pillowed between layers of vanilla ice cream.

In the early 1930s, Isaly's introduced its "Original Chipped Chopped Ham," a spicy pressed ham made in loaves. It was an immediate hit with customers, especially in Pittsburgh where workers and school children favored it in sandwiches they carried in their lunch boxes.

Sadly, Isaly's declined in the wake of supermarkets and the popularity of fast food restaurants. The firm, which included eleven dairy plants and 400 dairy stores by 1950, was sold in 1972. Sold again in 1977, it eventually went out of business.

Today, various companies manufacture Isaly products and are licensed to use the Isaly name.

Fortunately, Pittsburghers are still able to enjoy a true taste of tradition. Tom and Gail Weisbecker operate one of the few remaining, independently owned, Isaly's stores. They are located in West View, a northern suburb of Pittsburgh. The original (circa 1950) storefront has been preserved, attracting new customers as well as those who remember the Isaly's of their youth.

The Weisbecker's strive for authenticity inside, too, serving Isaly Chipped Chopped Ham and Isaly-brand ice cream to customers in the original four-seat booths. Tom mans the grill as well as the old chipper that has shaved the ham paper-thin since the 1930s. Gail waits on customers, serving up plenty of wit and personality along with the food, which rolls steadily out of the kitchen beginning at 6:00 A.M.

Basically, the Weisbeckers will serve chipped ham sandwiches just about any way their customers request, including a hearty special breakfast sandwich with ham, two eggs, cheese, lettuce, and tomato on a large bun. Folks stop by throughout the day for ice cream cones. And other customers come from as far away as Cincinnati and head to the deli counter where they load up on several pounds of ham and dozens of rolls that are taken home to those who crave a taste of years gone by.

Sandwich

Most Pittsburghers who grew up in the 1950s remember eating Isaly's Chipped Chopped Ham sandwiches. The preparation was pretty basic in those days. Marlene Parrish, a Pittsburgh food writer, reminisces about her two favorites: chipped ham piled on store-bought white bread and spread with tons of mayonnaise, or chipped ham heated with Heinz Ketchup and a little pickle relish (what Pittsburghers would call BBQ sauce) and served on white bread.

Today, the Isaly's Chipped Chopped Ham sandwich has been revised and updated. The ham is still sliced paper-thin, via a method called chipping, so that it piles up like pieces of silk. At Isaly's in West View, the Weisbeckers serve it in their signature sandwich called the "Slammer." A full half-pound of ham is grilled, topped with a choice of cheese (Swiss, cheddar, American, or provolone) and plenty of fried onions, all piled into a big soft roll freshly baked on premise. The sandwich has become a local favorite - producer Rick Seback of PBS affiliate WQED in Pittsburgh can frequently be spotted wolfing down a "Slammer" or two for lunch.

The Isaly Chipped Chopped Ham "Slammer"
Reprinted with permission from
Tom and Gail Weisbecker,
owners of Isaly's in West View, Pennsylvania.

1 medium onion, sliced, rings separated, and fried until nicely browned
Vegetable oil for grilling
½ pound Isaly's Chipped Chopped Ham or spiced, pressed ham, sliced or chipped
Cheese of choice (Swiss, cheddar, provolone or American)
1 large soft bun

Over medium heat, grill or fry the chipped chopped ham in a small amount of vegetable oil in a medium frying pan. Top with cheese, cover, and continue cooking just until the cheese melts. Place ham and cheese in a large soft bun, top with fried onions, and serve immediately. Yield: 1 sandwich.

Note: Ham similar to the Isaly's brand is sometimes sold as "old fashioned spiced ham."

Where to Go:

Isaly's
448 Perry Highway
West View, PA

SAUSAGE: A PROUD IMMIGRANT HERITAGE

Sausage making dates back at least to the beginning of agriculture and the domestication of animals in the Middle East. The Chinese may have known it as early as 5000 B.C. because, by that time, they had domesticated hogs. As civilization grew and flourished throughout the world, nearly every society developed some kind of sausage, and many of those sausages were eventually brought to America by the diverse immigrant groups who carried with them their culinary traditions and foodways. Today, there is hardly an ethnic group or a region in the United States that doesn't boast of at least one unique and special sausage.

Italian Sausage with Peppers & Onions

The largest wave of Italian immigrants to America began in the 1880s, with the majority settling in and around New York City and Philadelphia. In **No Foreign Food: The American Diet in Time and Place**, author Richard Pillsbury points out that Italian settlement branched out from those major population centers to encompass Pittsburgh and Chicago, and in New York State, settlement primarily followed the Erie Canal west to Buffalo.

Although Italian restaurants began appearing in these major cities around the 1890s, it wasn't until after World War II, when many servicemen returned home with a new appreciation for the cuisine, that Italian food became generally popular.

Because preserved meats had long been a specialty in Italy, Italian Americans naturally reproduced their beloved sausage products made from old country recipes, initially for their own consumption and then, increasingly, for sale to a more worldly public. Italian meat markets like Buffalo's Mineo & Sapio began springing up around the 1920s, and many more such establishments followed in the 1950s and 1960s. A type of pork sausage made into links and typically flavored with garlic and anise or fennel seed was a popular item and became generically known as "Italian sausage." The addition of hot red pepper flakes created the "hot" variety while the other was termed "sweet."

For years, Italian delicatessens and home cooks prepared sandwiches composed of Italian sausage topped with sautéed peppers or onions or a mix of both. It wasn't long before entrepreneurs began selling the popular sandwiches at church fund raisers and public events. Nancy and Arthur Hawkins note, in **The American Regional Cookbook**, that Italian sausages with peppers were served on rolls at New Jersey's Palisades Park, an amusement park that existed from 1898 to 1971.

Today, the enormously popular Italian sausage sandwiches are found throughout the Northeastern metropolitan areas of original Italian settlement as well as the Chicago area. They can be found at a variety of venues including ballgames, festivals, carnivals, and fairs.

Sandwich

The Italian sausage sandwich is composed of a grilled sweet or hot Italian sausage served on a crusty roll and generously topped with a mixture of grilled chopped onions and green and red bell peppers. When the Boston Red Sox are playing at home, at least one popular sausage vendor outside Fenway Park can be found selling Italian sausage injected with Dr Pepper – fans rave about it.

Italian Sausage with Peppers and Onions

1 tablespoon olive oil
2 large onions, halved and sliced into medium-sized strips
2 red bell peppers, sliced into medium-sized strips
2 green bell peppers, sliced into medium-sized strips
8 Italian sausages (hot or sweet)
8 sausage or hot dog rolls

In a medium-sized frying pan, heat the olive oil and add the onion. Sauté onions over medium heat until they just begin to soften. Add peppers and continue to sauté the mixture until vegetables are just beginning to soften and brown. Remove from heat and set aside.

Preheat grill and brush grid lightly with olive oil. Add sausages and grill until cooked through and golden brown.

Just before sausages are finished cooking, reheat the onions and peppers, allowing them to brown a bit more. When sausages are cooked, remove from grill or push them to one side. Place rolls facedown on grill and lightly toast them. Place sausages in the rolls, top with peppers and onions, and serve immediately. Yield: 8 sandwiches.

Where to Go:

George's Sandwiches
900¹/₂ South 9th Street
Philadelphia, PA

• • • • • • • • • • • • • • •

Need a Quick Fix?

Philadelphia's historic Italian Market is home to many purveyors of fine Italian food. D'Angelo Brothers sells a huge array of specialty sausages, including both sweet and hot Italian. Just call them for mail order.

D'Angelo Brothers Meat Market
909 South 9th Street
Philadelphia, PA 19147
Telephone: (215) 923-5637

Bratwurst

Sheboygan, Wisconsin, aka the "Wurst City in the World," is formally known as the "Bratwurst Capital of the World." Indeed, the city's bratwurst, a spicy, fresh pork sausage, is so popular throughout the state that the Wisconsin legislature declared a "Sheboygan double bratwurst on a hard roll, with the works…the ultimate state sandwich." And nowhere is the brat taken more seriously than in Sheboygan where an annual festival, Bratwurst Days, is held in its honor every August.

The bratwurst in America dates back to around 1890. Thousands of German immigrants made their way to Wisconsin and America's heartland, attracted by the lush agricultural lands, in the latter part of the nineteenth century. The region became known for its grain and hog production, facilitating the eventual establishment of the butcher shops and meat packing plants that are a hallmark of the region. Those Germans who settled in Wisconsin introduced bratwurst and a host of other traditional sausages. Although Sheboygan is noted for the sausage, with nearly a dozen meat markets specializing in bratwurst, it's also made in numerous locations throughout the state.

Sandwich

The original bratwurst is a delicately spiced, fresh pork sausage, but in recent years, manufacturers have introduced new varieties like onion, garlic, and jalapeño-cheddar bratwurst. Most bratwurst comes in a tubular casing, but sausage patties are also available. Wisconsinites recommend buying the fresh, or at least frozen-fresh bratwurst versus the pre-cooked type.

Many cooks advocate boiling the sausage in beer before grilling, while others flatly state the need to carefully grill it until the sausage is crusty on the outside and still juicy on the inside. Some taverns simply steam or poach their brats. Bratwurst fans are adamant about using crusty hard rolls, also of German origin, for construction of a brat sandwich. The official state version calls for two bratwurst on a single hard roll with mustard, onion, and pickles. Sauerkraut is another popular option.

Grilled Brats, Sheboygan Style

4 fresh bratwurst sausages
1 12-ounce bottle of beer (do not use "lite" beer)
4 bratwurst rolls, crusty rolls, or hot dog rolls
Softened butter
German or Dijon-style mustard (or mustard of choice)
Chopped fresh onion
Pickles (optional)
Sauerkraut (optional)

Pierce each bratwurst four times with a fork and place in a pan large enough to hold them in one layer. Add beer, bring to a boil over medium heat, and let simmer for 15 to 20 minutes.

Preheat grill and brush grid lightly with olive oil. Drain bratwurst and place on grill over medium-high heat. Grill bratwurst for about 10 minutes or until well browned.

Meanwhile, lightly butter the rolls. Just before brats are done, place rolls under a preheated broiler, or facedown on the grill, until they are golden brown. Place brats in rolls and serve with mustard, onion, and pickles or sauerkraut, if desired. Yield: 4 sandwiches.

Where to Go:

Visitors to Sheboygan, Wisconsin, will want to check out one or both of these eateries:

The Charcoal Inn
1637 Geele Avenue

Gosse's Drive-Thru
2928 N. 13th

● ● ● ● ● ● ● ● ● ● ● ● ● ● ●

Need A Quick Fix?

The Sheboygan Bratwurst Company will happily fulfill your every bratwurst wish, from original brats to onion, garlic, or japaleño-cheddar brats, and they'll even supply those famous hard rolls. Visit their web site for information, then call or fax your order.

Sheboygan Bratwurst Company
P.O. Box 276
Sheboygan, WI 53082-0276
Web Site: http://www.bratwurst.net
Telephone: (888) 966-6966
Fax: (920) 803-5190

Americans have always eaten cheese. From the arrival of the first immigrants until the mid-nineteenth century, cheese was made at home by farmwives or by small producers in what amounted to a cottage industry. The first cheddar cheese factory in the United States was built in Oneida County, New York, in 1851. In the past thirty years, United States annual domestic consumption of cheese has more than doubled, and it's now at thirty pounds per person. American cheese eaters can select from over 300 domestic varieties as well as an untold number of imports, and increasingly sophisticated tastes encompass artisanal and specialty cheeses, many of which make their appearance in sandwiches.

Pimiento Cheese Sandwich

Pimiento cheese is a favorite sandwich filling and specialty of the American South, where it's referred to as "Southern comfort food." It is purchased off grocery shelves or, more likely, made fresh at home.

While the South is not known historically for its cheese production, simply because it wasn't possible to easily store it until the advent of refrigeration, **Mrs. Hill's Southern Practical Cookery and Receipt Book**, published in 1867, does provide detailed instructions for making cheese. "Annotta," as it was then called, was used to impart a yellow color to the cheese, and Mrs. Hill recommended mixing red pepper with butter to be used for greasing the outside of the cheese, thus discouraging flies (another food hazard in those days). Known today as annatto, it's made from achiote seed and, in the United States, it's

referred to as "butter coloring" because it's commonly used to color both butter and cheddar cheese. Perhaps Mrs. Hill's old receipt eventually provided the inspiration for pimiento cheese, which has typically been identified with the South.

Mrs. S.R. Dull provided a recipe for "Open Pimiento Toast" in **Southern Cooking**, originally published in 1928. Mrs. Dull was a well known food authority in her day, having worked for the *Atlanta Journal* as editor of the Home Economics page, and was referred to as "the first lady of cooking in Georgia and the outstanding culinary expert of the South." Her recipe instructs the cook to trim the crust from whole wheat bread and toast it. Butter and pimiento cheese are spread on the toast, the slice is cut into three pieces, and then placed in a hot oven until the cheese begins to melt. She advocates serving the toast with coffee, commenting that it is "nice for a last course at dinner."

This dainty savory was most likely the precursor of the hearty pimiento cheese sandwich that became popular during the Depression. In **A Gracious Plenty**, John T. Edge notes that pimiento cheese became popular coincident with the country store and the availability of hoop cheese. And as Joseph E. Dabney points out in his informative book **Smokehouse Ham, Spoon Bread, & Scuppernong Wine**, yellow cheese was most certainly made in the remote Appalachian Highlands of the 1920s and 1930s where nothing, including milk from Bossie the cow, went to waste.

While no one has yet discovered the true origin of pimiento cheese, many Southern food writers quote author Reynolds Price, whose comments appeared in the 1981 **Great American Writers' Cookbook**. Price notes his failure in an extensive effort to discover its origin, but he does recall it as "the peanut butter of his childhood," homemade by his mother. Price was born in 1933 in Macon, North Carolina, indicating that pimiento cheese was undoubtedly a well-established food by the 1930s.

In "Gittin' Back to My Roots", Roger Hudson of Charlotte, North Carolina, notes that his grandmother believed pimiento cheese originated during the Depression as a "poor man's food," an excellent sandwich filling for men like his grandfather working on CCC or WPA projects. During the 1930s, pimientos were only ten cents a can, and Roger recalls that the Ashe County Cheese Company, then owned by Kraft, in Ashe County, North Carolina, was producing hoop cheese as far back as 1930, making it a leading supplier during the Depression. But Hudson says his mother made pimiento cheese by grating American or cheddar cheese, rather than hoop cheese, and adding mayonnaise, a can of pimientos, and a dash of salt and pepper. He also remembers his grandmother referring to it as "minner cheese," and he quotes her as saying, "Do you'ns want a minner cheese sandwich?" Others, he believes, may well have called it "puh-minter" cheese.

Apparently, pimiento cheese was also known North of the Mason-Dixon line in one form or another. Eva Greene Fuller included a recipe for a "Pimento (sic) Sandwich" in **The Up-to-date Sandwich Book** published in 1909 by A. C. McClurg & Co. of Chicago. A company known for its American editions of British imprints, by the late 1800s McClurg had also established a stable of Midwest writers, a group that perhaps included Fuller. Her recipe calls for grinding canned pimentos (sic) with cakes of Neufchatel cheese, similar to cream cheese, and quite different from the tart-sour taste of the hoop cheese often credited with popularizing pimiento cheese in the South. Even Californians were familiar with the pimiento cheese sandwich, as evidenced by its appearance on a 1930 menu from The Hotel Barbara Worth in El Centro.

By 1946, the pimiento cheese sandwich had become mainstream throughout the United States, evidenced by Florence Brobeck's recipe for a "Snappy Cheese and Pimiento" sandwich in **The Lunch Box and Every Kind of Sandwich**.

Sandwich

In today's South, pimiento cheese is just as likely to make its appearance as a topping on hot dogs and hamburgers as a filling for sandwiches. Beth Tartan, author of **North Carolina & Old Salem Cookery**, points out that while some folks make their pimiento cheese in a double boiler, the uncooked version is the most popular.

Pimiento cheese is still typically made from grated cheddar or American cheese mixed with mayonnaise, canned pimientos, salt, and pepper. However, there are probably as many variations as there are cooks, with suggested additions including mustard, hot red pepper sauce, chopped green onion, garlic, lemon juice, horseradish, wine, or Worcestershire sauce. Pimiento cheese is traditionally spread on white bread, but variations include wheat or rye.

Pimiento Cheese Sandwich

10-ounces sharp cheddar cheese, grated
1 4-ounce jar pimientos, drained
1/2 cup mayonnaise
1 tablespoon lemon juice
1 teaspoon Worcestershire sauce
1/8 teaspoon cayenne pepper (or more, to taste)
16 slices good quality sandwich bread (white, wheat, or rye)
Additional mayonnaise (optional)

In a mixing bowl, combine cheese, pimientos, mayonnaise, lemon juice, Worcestershire sauce, and cayenne pepper. Mix well with a fork, mashing the mixture a bit to create a chunky-style spread. Store in a tightly covered container, and refrigerate for several hours or overnight, allowing flavors to blend. Just before serving, spread 1/4 cup pimiento cheese on each of 8 slices of bread. If desired, spread a thin coating of mayonnaise on each of the remaining eight slices of bread. Top each pimiento cheese-covered slice with a second slice of bread, cut sandwich in half, and serve immediately. Yield: 2 cups pimiento cheese or 8 sandwiches.

Note: Spreading pimiento cheese on hot toasted bread produces a creamier sandwich. Crisply fried and drained bacon is a non-traditional but delicious variation. Pimiento cheese can also be used as a spread for crackers or as a topping for hot dogs and hamburgers as featured at the Varsity in Atlanta, Georgia.

Where to Go:

Recommended is John T. Edge's definitive book *Southern Belly*, which provides information on where to find all kinds of real Southern food along with eloquent social commentary. Obviously a fan of pimiento cheese, Edge reveals several dining spots where a "P.C." sandwich is featured. Len Berg's, established in 1908, is a Macon, Georgia, institution. Sally Bell's Kitchen in Richmond, Virginia, is a bakery famous for its box lunches that include killer potato salad, deviled eggs, and sandwiches made on homemade bread.

Len Berg's
240 Old Post Office Alley
Macon, GA

Sally Bell's Kitchen
708 W. Grace Street
Richmond, VA

Grilled Cheese Sandwiches

To most Americans, there's nothing more comforting than a grilled cheese sandwich. With the plethora of new cheeses now available on the market, we are continually discovering new combinations and taste sensations, but the classic grilled cheese remains number one in the hearts of many.

Charles Hollister Moore's Grilled Cheese Sandwich

Holly Moore is an expert on where to find the best chow in America, and he generously shares the results of his extensive research on his web site http://www.HollyEats.com. Holly's dad was famous for this terrific sandwich – one bite will tell you why!

2 slices of white bread
Butter
Thick slices of aged cheddar cheese
Sliced tomatoes
Sliced baked ham

Butter one side of each slice of bread. On the unbuttered side of one slice of bread, layer remaining ingredients in the order given. Top with remaining slice of bread, buttered side up. Grill sandwich on an old-fashioned waffle iron; Belgian irons won't work. Yield: 1 sandwich.

Holly's Note: Along with producing a great-tasting sandwich, the waffle iron creates a handy grid for eating the sandwich in a straight line. Also, the cheese that seeps out of the sandwich and weaves around the grid on the waffle iron will toast up nice and crispy, and it's delicious all by itself!

Where to Go:

Wolf's Market at 1500 Locust Street in Philadelphia, Pennsylvania, is a trendy, upscale food store that features popular take-out items. Described as a visual as well as a taste experience, Wolf's has a great sandwich counter that includes both hot and cold choices. Their grilled cheese sandwich, made on extra-thick Texas toast, boasts a substantial layer of cheddar cheese and thick tomato slices.

TROTTIN' OUT THE TURKEY - ALL GUSSIED UP!

Americans are eating more turkey. In years gone by, it was served mainly on holidays, but our national consumption of the bird has more than doubled over the past twenty-five years. Convenience and versatility have resulted in its appearance in many new forms, including turkey burgers and sausage. Turkey has long been featured as an elegant ingredient in many of our most popular sandwiches, and the National Turkey Federation reports increased consumption of turkey sandwiches outside the home. Curiously, June, rather than November, is National Turkey Lovers' Month.

The Hot Brown

A chef named Fred K. Schmidt who worked at Louisville's Brown Hotel devised the legendary Hot Brown Sandwich so favored by Kentuckians. When it first opened in 1923, the hotel's nightly dinner dances drew more than 1200 guests. At the end of the evening, people in search of something to eat would head for the dining room. It wasn't long before they tired of the usual ham and eggs, and when Chef Schmidt produced The Hot Brown, an open-face turkey sandwich bathed in a delicate cheese sauce, society was delighted and a tradition was born. The sandwich became so popular that it spread throughout Kentucky and even beyond state borders. Back at the Brown Hotel, it was also featured on the regular menu where it became a favorite of the "ladies who lunch" crowd.

Well known Southern food writer Marion Flexner wrote in her 1949 **Out of Kentucky Kitchens** that, in those days, the Brown Hotel offered two sandwich specials, both known as a "Brown Sandwich" but with one served cold and the other hot. Indeed, the Brown Hotel has in its archives an old menu from the 1930s that lists both the "Cold Brown" at $1.25 and the "Hot Brown" at $1.50. The cold version, generally offered in the summer, was composed of a single slice of rye bread on which slices of chicken or turkey, lettuce, a slice of tomato, and hard-boiled egg slices were piled. Thousand Island dressing was served "to douse all over the sandwich." The hot version, which Flexner notes was more popular, was closer to what we know today as The Hot Brown, and it was based on a slice of toast covered with sliced chicken or turkey, cheese sauce, and bacon strips, sprinkled with grated Parmesan cheese, and broiled until golden brown. The Hot Brown continues to be revered as part of Kentucky's culinary heritage, and recipes for the sandwich, in numerous variations, are common in Kentucky fund raising cookbooks.

Although The Hot Brown is listed on many a restaurant menu in the upper South, perhaps the best place to sample it is at The Camberley Brown Hotel in Louisville. Built in 1923 by local philanthropist J. Graham Brown, the hotel has served as a major center for Louisville social life since it's opening. Today, The Thoroughbred Lounge in The Camberley Brown Hotel lists the sandwich on its menu as "The Hot Brown."

Sandwich

While there are lots of different recipes given for The Hot Brown, they always include a rich cheese sauce, sometimes made from cheddar or Swiss. The sandwich is commonly composed of one or two slices of toasted white bread topped with thin slices of turkey or chicken, country ham or crisp bacon, and sliced tomato. Covered with cheese sauce and sprinkled with Parmesan cheese, the sandwich is baked until bubbling hot and then quickly browned under the broiler.

The Hot Brown
Reprinted with permission from The Camberley Brown Hotel, Louisville, Kentucky.

Sauce:
1/2 **cup butter**
1/2 **cup flour**
4 **cups milk**
6 **tablespoons grated Parmesan cheese**
1 **beaten egg at room temperature**
1 **ounce whipped cream (optional)**
Salt and pepper to taste

12 **slices of white bread, toasted**
2 1/2 - 3 **pounds sliced roast turkey**
Additional Parmesan cheese for topping

12 **strips of bacon, cooked crisp and drained**

In a large saucepan, melt butter over medium heat. Whisk in flour to make a thick roux. Whisking constantly, gradually add the milk, and cook slowly, whisking frequently, for 5 to 10 minutes to remove any taste of raw flour. Whisk in the Parmesan cheese, and let the mixture cool slightly. Add the egg to thicken the sauce, but do not allow the sauce to boil or it will curdle. Remove from heat, and fold in whipped cream if desired. Season the sauce with salt and pepper to taste. Set aside and keep warm.

Preheat broiler. For each Hot Brown, place two slices of toast on a metal or flameproof dish. Cover the toast with a liberal amount of turkey. Pour a generous amount of sauce over the turkey and the toast. Sprinkle with additional grated Parmesan cheese. Place the entire dish under the broiler until the sauce is speckled brown and bubbly. Remove from broiler, cross two pieces of bacon over the top, and serve immediately. Yield: 6 sandwiches.

Note: Cissy Gregg, Food Editor for **The Courier-Journal** in Louisville from 1942 until the early 1960s, recommended using 1/2 cup grated cheddar and 1/2 cup grated Parmesan for the preparation of what she called the Louisville Hot Brown.

The Camberley Brown Hotel
The Thoroughbred Lounge
335 West Broadway
Louisville, KY

Devonshire Sandwich

Pittsburgh restaurateur Frank Blandi created the Devonshire sandwich in 1934 when he opened his first dining establishment, The Stratford, in the North Oakland area. For the Blandi family, owners of a New York wine business that failed following Prohibition, the move to Pittsburgh was fortuitous, and they proceeded to open additional restaurants, including the St. Moritz Hotel in East Liberty, the dining room at the Pittsburgh Playhouse, Park Schenley, and Le Mont.

Blandi's creation, supposedly named for Pittsburgh's Devonshire Street, remains a favorite in a city known for its hearty, delicious sandwiches.

Sandwich

The original Devonshire was composed of slices of turkey and crisp bacon layered on a slice of toast, covered with a rich cheese sauce, and baked in a hot oven until golden and bubbly. Although Pittsburgh has seen lots of change since the 1930s, the Devonshire sandwich recipe has remained the same.

The Original Devonshire Sandwich

Reprinted with permission from Marlene Parrish, food writer for the *Pittsburgh Post-Gazette* and numerous national magazines.

Cream sauce:
6 tablespoons butter, melted
1 cup flour
2 cups chicken broth
2 cups hot milk
1 teaspoon salt
½ teaspoon ground black pepper (optional)
4 ounces Cheddar cheese, grated

For each sandwich:
1 slice good quality toast, crusts trimmed off
3 slices bacon, cooked crisp and drained
5 thin slices cooked turkey breast (about 3 – 4 ounces per serving)
Cream sauce (recipe above)
Melted butter (about 4 tablespoons)
Grated Parmesan cheese
Paprika

Cream sauce: In a large saucepan, melt the butter over medium heat, and mix in the flour – it will be very thick. Whisking constantly, add the chicken broth and then the hot milk and salt. Simmer over low heat for 10 to 20 minutes, stirring frequently. Add cheese and stir to melt thoroughly. Cool to lukewarm. Whisk again until smooth before using. Thin the sauce with additional milk if necessary. This makes enough sauce for six Devonshire sandwiches.

Assembly: Preheat oven to 450°. In each individual, flat ovenproof casserole dish, place one slice of toast and top with 3 slices of bacon. Add 5 thin slices of cooked turkey breast. Cover completely with cream sauce. Sprinkle with a little melted butter, then sprinkle with grated Parmesan cheese and paprika. Bake 10 to 15 minutes or until golden brown. Yield: 1 sandwich.

Where to Go:

Union Grill
413 S. Craig Street
Pittsburgh, PA

The Elena Ruz Sandwich

In Florida, Cuban immigrants and their descendants enjoy a different kind of turkey sandwich, and it's gaining a big following among all who discover it. It's known as the Elena Ruz or, sometimes, the Elena Ruth sandwich. Two different stories are told about its Cuban origin in the days before Castro. According to the first version, there was a man who always took his little daughter to lunch at a popular Havana restaurant on Saturdays. Because she was a fussy eater, it was difficult to find something on the menu that she liked. Finally, knowing that his daughter was fond of strawberry jam, the man asked the waiter to create a sandwich based on it, and the result was the Elena Ruth, named after the little girl.

But the second story seems to be the true version, and it was uncovered by Fabiola Santiago of **The Miami Herald** who interviewed the real Elena Ruz, then 87 years old, in 1996. Ruz told of the days when, as a young socialite in the 1930s, she and her friends frequently lunched at El Carmelo in the upscale Vedado section of Havana. Ruz said that she always ordered the same sandwich, a combination that she had created based on cream cheese and strawberry jam spread on toasted medianoche bread (a Cuban-style egg roll) and topped with sliced roast turkey. After a friend told Ruz that she had dreamed the sandwich would make her famous, Ruz asked the restaurant to put it on the menu so she wouldn't always have to instruct the wait staff on its preparation. The sandwich became so popular that Cuban immigrants brought it to Miami when they fled their homeland upon Castro's assumption of power in 1959.

Most Cuban restaurant menus in the Miami area include the Elena Ruz or Elena Ruth sandwich. Felipe Valls, Sr., who fled Cuba in 1960, founded La Carreta Restaurant, and today, La Carreta Restaurants are scattered throughout the Miami area. Known for its upscale version of Cuban fast food, La Carreta features the Elena Ruth sandwich on its menu.

Elena Ruz Sandwich

1 soft medianoche (egg) roll or
2 slices white bread, toasted
Cream cheese, softened
Strawberry jam
4 ounces thinly sliced roasted turkey breast

Spread one slice of the bread or egg roll with cream cheese and then spread with strawberry jam. Top with sliced turkey breast, then cover with the second slice of bread or the top of the roll. The real Elena Ruz did not eat her sandwich pressed and grilled like a Cuban sandwich is served (see Cuban Sandwich). Today, however, the Elena Ruz is served either grilled or plain. It can also be placed in a warm oven until slightly crispy if desired.
Yield: 1 sandwich.

Where to Go:

La Carreta serves the Elena Ruz (listed on the menu as the Elena Ruth), at its eight restaurants, including the one at 3632 Southwest Eighth Street (Calle Ocho) in Miami, Florida.

Monte Cristo

It is generally said that the Monte Cristo sandwich was created in California, but thereafter, details are pretty sketchy. One such story generally credits its development to San Francisco in the 1950s, while another specifically states it originated at the Coronado Hotel in San Diego, but no date is provided. In her **West Coast Cook Book,** published in 1952, Helen Evans Brown notes that the Monte Cristo (made from sliced chicken or turkey) and Monte Carlo (made from sliced tongue) sandwiches had recently become very popular, and she thought they originated in San Francisco. However, a recipe for the Monte Cristo is given in **The Brown Derby Cookbook,** published in 1949, and the sandwich is also listed on a 1941 menu from Gordon's, a restaurant that was located on Wilshire Boulevard in Los Angeles, evidence that the sandwich certainly predates the 1950s. In true California style, the name may have been inspired by the popular 1934 "Monte Cristo" film. Unfortunately, no one seems to really know who was definitively responsible for developing it or what establishment may be entitled to credit.

Sandwich authorities believe that the Monte Cristo is a California version of the grilled cheese sandwich, a long time American favorite based on the French *croque monsieur*. The Monte Cristo was originally served as a luncheon dish or an after-theater snack. According to Helen Evans Brown, the Monte Cristo or the Monte Carlo sandwiches, cut into one-inch squares, were called Monte Benitos and served with cocktails.

While California may, indeed, rightly claim the Monte Cristo as we know it today, it must be pointed out that the Browns give a recipe for a "Club Sandwich," attributed to New York, in **America Cooks: Favorite Recipes from the 48 States** that sounds suspiciously like the basis for a Monte Cristo. In the Browns' recipe, which dates from 1937, white bread encases sliced ham, Swiss cheese, and sliced chicken breast, the sandwich is soaked in a mixture of beaten egg and heavy cream, and then fried. And in **Fashionable Food,** Sylvia Lovegren gives a recipe for "Cheese Dreams," a term used for grilled cheese sandwiches in the 1930s, and points out that it is similar to a Monte Cristo since the cheese sandwich is dipped in a mixture of egg and milk and fried in butter until golden. The recipe appeared in Proctor & Gamble's 1937 Crisco cookbook.

Today, Monte Cristo sandwiches are featured on restaurant menus throughout the country. The restaurant most famous for its Monte Cristo is probably the Blue Bayou Restaurant at Disney Land in Anaheim, California, where it has been served since 1966.

Sandwich

Two slices of white bread are typically filled with ham, turkey, and a slice of Swiss cheese. The sandwich is dipped in beaten egg, deep-fried in vegetable oil, dusted with confectioner's sugar, and served with a side of jam for dipping. The Monte Cristo can also be dipped in batter before it's deep-fried; fans seem to be equally divided relative to their preference for egg or batter dip.

Monte Cristo

Batter:
1½ cups all-purpose flour
2 teaspoons baking powder
¼ teaspoon salt
Pinch of cayenne (red) pepper
2 large eggs, beaten
1½ cups milk

For each sandwich:
2 slices good quality white bread
Dijon-style mustard
2 very thin slices deli-style Virginia baked ham
1 thin slice Swiss cheese
1 – 2 thin slices American cheese
2 very thin slices deli-style roast turkey breast

Vegetable oil for frying
Powdered sugar
Strawberry or raspberry jam

Batter: Make batter one hour prior to use. In a large bowl, mix together flour, baking powder, salt, and cayenne pepper. Whisk together the beaten egg and the milk, then whisk it into the flour mixture until well combined and all lumps have disappeared. Cover and set aside until ready to use. Yield: Enough batter for 6 sandwiches.

Sandwich assembly: Lightly spread Dijon-style mustard on one side of each piece of bread. Add remaining ingredients in order listed, making sure that any over-hang of ingredients is trimmed or tucked into the sandwich. Top with remaining slice of bread. Lay sandwich on a flat surface and cover with a cutting board, pressing down lightly to compress sandwich.

In a deep, medium-sized frying pan, add oil to a depth of one-half inch, and heat oil to 375°. Whisk batter. Dip sandwich into batter, covering thoroughly and letting any excess batter drip off. Carefully immerse sandwich into hot oil, and fry, turning once, for about 3 minutes total or until dark golden brown. Remove sandwich from oil and drain on paper towels. Place sandwich on a serving plate, cut into four pieces, lightly sift top with powdered sugar, and serve immediately with jam of choice for dipping. Yield: 1 sandwich.

SANDWICHES WITH "THE WORKS"

Americans have always had a fondness for glitz and excess, and that predilection can even be found in some of our favorite sandwiches. Piled high with what some would describe as "everything but the kitchen sink," these sandwiches can be as intimidating as they are delicious. But in the end, the message is not lost: these sandwiches are fun, and they provide the ultimate in comfort food.

Horseshoe & Ponyshoe Sandwich

The horseshoe sandwich was created in 1928 at the old Leland Hotel in Springfield, Illinois. It was so named due to the shape of the ham cut that, at one time, was used in making this open-faced sandwich. The French fries that top the sandwich are said to represent the nails in a horseshoe. A ponyshoe sandwich is simply half of a horseshoe sandwich.

Springfield residents and visitors looking for a good horseshoe sandwich tend to head for the Norb Andy Tabarin. Virgil Hickox, a prominent citizen of the time, constructed the building as a home in 1839. After Hickox's death in 1881, the building was used for a number of different purposes. In 1937, Norbert Anderson established The Norb Andy Tabern in the portion of the building that is below street level (tabern is a Persian word referring to a public place with tables). A favorite gathering spot for politicians and the press, Norb Andy's, as it's locally known, has long been a favorite place for enjoying

Springfield's famous horseshoe sandwich.

Sandwich

These days, a standard horseshoe sandwich is likely to be made from two hamburgers or a generous mound of turkey atop two slices of toasted white bread. Ham or a combination of turkey, ham, and hamburger, are alternative combinations. A hearty, rich cheese sauce is poured over the meat and a generous mound of French fries crowns this culinary glory of Springfield.

Horseshoe Sandwich

Cheese sauce:
2 tablespoons butter
2 tablespoons flour
¼ teaspoon salt
¼ teaspoon ground pepper
1 cup milk
3 cups grated cheddar cheese

4 slices of white bread, toasted
4 hamburger patties, cooked as desired
1 pound hot, freshly cooked French fries

In a medium saucepan, melt butter over medium heat and whisk in the flour. Whisking constantly, add the milk. Add the cheese in three batches, whisking until each addition is melted. Bring mixture just to the boiling point, lower heat, and cook 5 minutes, whisking constantly. Set aside and keep warm.

Place two slices of toast on each of two large plates. Cover each slice of toast with a cooked hamburger patty. Pour sauce over the patties, dividing it evenly. Top each plate with a mound of French fries and serve immediately.
Yield: 2 servings.

Where to Go:

Norb Andy Tabarin
518 E. Capitol
Springfield, IL

The Primanti Sandwich

In the 1920s, the Primanti family opened a late night diner located in Pittsburgh's "Strip District," so-called because it's actually a narrow strip of land confined by the natural boundaries of Grant's Hill to the south and the Allegheny River to the north. From the beginning, Primanti's was destined to become a Pittsburgh institution.

The 1920s was a time of great prosperity for businesses in the Strip District, which was populated by numerous produce merchants, industrial concerns, shops, and private residences. The Primanti Brothers' goal was to offer tasty, satisfying food in simple surroundings, a factor that not only ensured the success of their business early on but which carried them through the difficult years of the Depression and World War II. The eventual result was the creation of the Primanti sandwich, which is a complete meal served between two slices of bread.

The original Primanti Brothers on 18th Street is a 24-hour-per-day, 7-days-per-week operation, catering to folks looking for late night snacks, early morning breakfast, and serving as a popular lunch spot. It's in an area that has now become known for its retail food businesses, including produce and ethnic food purveyors, as well as for its numerous restaurants. But Primanti's stands head and shoulders above the crowd. Just ask anyone in Pittsburgh where to get a hearty sandwich and they'll immediately give directions to the nearest Primanti's. According to company officials, they sell 6,000 to 10,000 sandwiches in a good week.

Sandwich

The Primanti sandwich is a jaw-defying monstrosity served on waxed paper. A choice of meat, accompanied by provolone cheese, tomatoes, coleslaw, and French fries (onions are optional) are all piled in between two slabs of freshly baked Italian bread. According to one company employee, sandwiches are cut in half only for women and only upon request. Real men apparently don't need such frivolities.

Primanti Brothers' web site continually polls their customer's favorite sandwich, a categorization based on the choice of meat. Cheese steak leads the pack, followed by pastrami, capicolla, roast beef, corned beef, chicken, sausage, ham, and eggs.

Primanti-Style Pastrami Sandwich

1 tablespoon vegetable oil
6 ounces thinly sliced pastrami
1-2 slices provolone cheese
2 slices Italian bread
2 cups hot, freshly cooked French fries
½ cup coleslaw
2 slices of fresh tomato

Heat oil in a small skillet over medium high heat. Add pastrami and fry lightly on both sides just enough to heat it through. Combine pastrami into a single pile and top with provolone. Cover pan, turn heat to low, and cook just until the cheese begins to melt. With a spatula, remove

pastrami and cheese to one slice of the Italian bread. Add French fries, coleslaw, and tomatoes. Top with the second slice of bread and serve immediately. Yield: 1 very large sandwich.

Where to Go:

Primanti Brothers has six locations in the Pittsburgh area, including:

46 W. 18th Street at Smallman in the Strip District
and
19th at Carson on the Southside (WQED producer Rick Sebak's favorite)

Garbage Plate™

Nick Tahou Hots in Rochester, New York, is the home of the one and only "Garbage Plate™," an all-encompassing sandwich plate that includes meat and several sides. It's considered de rigueur to head for Nick's after a night on the town – a garbage plate can be a very sobering experience.

Nick's, as it's locally known, was established in 1918 by Alexander Tahou. The original "Garbage Plate" followed shortly thereafter, but at that time, it was called "Hots and Potatoes." In those days, two hot dogs would be accompanied by a choice of either cold baked beans or home fries, a meal that kept many a working man well fed at a reasonable price, especially during the Depression.

While the choice of sides was expanded over the years, Nick's continued with the original moniker until the early 1980s when college kids insisted upon ordering "the plate with all that garbage on it." The Tahou's natural resistance to the term "garbage" was finally overcome when they realized the marketability of the term. "Garbage Plate" was trademarked, and word of the unique "sandwich" has spread across the country.

Sandwich

A typical Garbage Plate™, served up on a heavy cardboard plate, is usually composed of two hot dogs or cheeseburgers cradled in optional rolls. Other selections include sausage, steak, fish, and eggs. Diners then have a choice of two sides: home fries, macaroni salad, French fries, or cold or hot baked beans. Current owner Alex Tahou says that home fries and macaroni salad are the most popular. The plate is then topped off with mustard, raw onions, and the Tahous' secret hot sauce.

Where to Go:

Nick Tahou Hots
320 W. Main Street
and
2260 Lyell Avenue
Rochester, NY

GREAT SANDWICHES FROM HUMBLE BEGINNINGS

You can't get much more basic than either eggs or beans, both of which have long formed the basis for countless dishes of renown in cuisines all over the world. In the United States, eggs and beans are natural showcase ingredients for any number of tasty sandwiches.

The St. Paul Sandwich

The St. Paul sandwich is another curiosity of St. Louis, a city with a penchant for creating odd sandwiches like those made with brains or snoots and ears. While one might assume that a sandwich with the moniker of "St. Paul" would have originated in Minnesota, most food authorities claim that it has nothing whatsoever to do with that area. Rather, they say, it's a noted specialty of many of the Chinese restaurants in the St. Louis, Missouri, area.

Interestingly, however, a St. Paul Sandwich is included in the 1940 **America Cooks: Favorite Recipes from the 48 States** by the Browns who attribute the sandwich to the Irish and the Swedes who settled in Minnesota. The version of the sandwich documented by the Browns consists of ham, onion, green pepper, and sweet pickles, all chopped and combined with beaten egg, fried, and served on toast with lettuce and olives. It brings to mind a rather interesting version of a Denver or Western sandwich.

The origin of today's St. Paul sandwich may be an enigma, but reports say that it was a popular offering in St. Louis as far back as the 1960s and perhaps earlier. Most folks, including St. Louis writer Thomas Crone, believe that Chinese restaurateurs who wanted to tempt the sandwich-loving American palate created it. This theory maintains that the sandwich is based on egg foo yung, an old Chinese recipe that has become thoroughly Americanized.

In **The Thousand Recipe Chinese Cookbook**, Gloria Bley Miller explains that the original or classic egg foo yung was actually a soufflé-like dish based on egg whites and minced chicken breast. Westernized versions of egg foo yung are based on scrambled whole eggs and various fillings. The home-style, or pan-fried version, is similar to an omelet whereas the restaurant version, ladled into hot oil, is deep-fried. Clearly, the St. Paul utilizes the latter method of preparation, making it a truly Chinese-American dish.

Sandwich

Plain old commercial white bread provides the underpinnings for the St. Paul sandwich. Then comes an egg foo yung patty, typically composed of eggs, onion, and bamboo shoots and enhanced with plenty of salt or MSG. Unlike egg foo yung, however, the combination is not scrambled but deep-fried. The bread is generously slathered with mayonnaise, and the egg foo yung patty is added along with pickle, tomato, and lettuce.

For those who want to take their St. Paul a step beyond the "plain" version, there are various additions available like shrimp, beef, chicken, pork, and ham. A "special" generally calls for three additional ingredients chosen from the list of options. Wrapped in white butcher's paper and encased in a brown paper bag, the St. Paul is an inexpensive moveable feast in a land of sandwich takeout options.

St. Paul Sandwich

3 eggs
$1/2$ teaspoon salt or MSG
$1/2$ cup diced cooked chicken breast
$1/2$ cup diced cooked ham
$1/4$ cup finely chopped green bell pepper
$1/4$ cup finely chopped onion
$1/2$ cup finely chopped bamboo shoots
$1/2$ cup finely chopped water chestnuts

Oil for deep-frying

6 slices plain white bread
Mayonnaise
Lettuce
3 thin slices of tomato
Pickle slices (optional)

Beat the eggs, and season with salt or MSG. Add meat and vegetables, and mix well. Set aside.

In a deep frying pan or pot, add oil to $1/4$ inch in depth. Heat oil over medium-high heat. Using a ladle, carefully but quickly add $1/2$ cup of egg mixture to oil. Baste the top of the patty with hot oil so it browns, and then, with a slotted spoon, flip the patty over, being careful not to splatter the oil. When golden brown on both sides, remove patty, drain on paper towels, and keep warm while frying remaining patties.

To assemble sandwiches, spread three slices of bread with mayonnaise to taste. Layer each with a slice of lettuce, an egg foo yung patty, a tomato slice, and pickles (optional). Cover with remaining slices of bread and serve immediately.
Yield: 3 sandwiches.

Note: Onion rolls are a delicious, non-traditional, substitute for white bread.

Where to Go:

Kim Van Restaurant
2649 Gravois Avenue
St. Louis, MO

Denver (Western) Sandwich

The **American Heritage Cookbook and Illustrated History of American Eating & Drinking** states that the Western sandwich was created by pioneers on the long trek west as a way to disguise the taste of eggs that had gone bad. Supposedly, the eggs were mixed with onion and other seasonings that might have been at hand. One wonders about this theory since most wagons, too heavily loaded to begin with, had to ditch valuable provisions early on. Eggs would have necessarily been cradled in straw or hay to prevent breakage and packed in heavy barrels designed to endure transport over barely recognizable trails. Surely, they would have been among the first provisions to be eaten or discarded.

Cora, Rose, and Bob Brown present a slightly different variation of this story in **America Cooks: Favorite Recipes from the 48 States**. They note that the Denver Sandwich "was born in covered wagon days, when eggs had to be hauled in over long hot trails." This supposedly refers to the transport of provisions to established settlements, not to pioneer wagons loaded down with people and household goods. Nevertheless, the result was the same: the eggs got so high by the time they were delivered that they had to be disguised with onion. At any rate, this explanation seems a bit more plausible.

Another theory proposes that chuck wagon cooks may have invented the Western sandwich to be carried as a snack in cowboy's saddlebags. Indeed, the Browns mention Ham Toast, or what they call "the great-grandaddy of the Denver sandwich," as a favorite of early cowboys. It was composed of finely chopped ham fried with pepper and eggs, then spread on hot toast.

A fourth theory says that the Denver sandwich was invented by Chinese cooks attempting to Americanize egg foo yung which, in its classical version, was a light soufflé made with egg whites and minced chicken breast, not at all like the hearty egg foo yung combinations now familiar to Americans. Indeed, the Chinese have long been known for the versatility of their egg cookery. According to James Beard in **American Cookery**, both eggs foo yung and the Denver or Western sandwich originated with Chinese cooks who manned the stoves for logging camps and railroad gangs in the nineteenth and early twentieth centuries. Quite possibly, the development of the Western sandwich paralleled that of the St. Paul sandwich, with both devised by enterprising Chinese cooks anxious to adapt their repertoire to American foods and tastes. And while we may never confirm the true origin of the Denver (Western) sandwich, contemplating the various possibilities is an interesting and fun culinary exercise.

The basic method of preparing the sandwich is based on that of an omelet, and it was first known as a "Denver omelet." Most likely, the preparation of the Denver sandwich, or Western, as it is commonly known in the East, changed and evolved over the years, eventually becoming the quintessential breakfast sandwich.

Unlike the "Denver Sandwich Bar," a once-popular candy bar that is no longer manufactured, the Denver, or Western, sandwich is still very much alive on restaurant menus across the country. It is commonly listed as a specialty of the house in Denver, Colorado, eating establishments. In diner lingo, the Denver or Western is known as a "cowboy."

Sandwich

The basic Denver, or Western, sandwich is composed of an omelet made with diced ham, onions, and green pepper. It's typically served on buttered toast made from white, rye, or whole wheat bread. A popular option in some areas is the inclusion of cheese, either mixed in the omelet or melted on top before it's served on toast.

Denver (Western) Sandwich

Filling:
1½ tablespoons butter
1½ tablespoons chopped green bell pepper
2 tablespoons chopped onion
¼ cup cubed ham

Omelet:
2 eggs
1 tablespoon water or milk
1 tablespoon butter

2 slices white, rye, or whole wheat bread, toasted and buttered
Salt and pepper to taste

Filling: In a small frying pan, melt the 1½ tablespoons butter over medium heat. Add the green pepper, onion, and ham, and sauté until vegetables are tender. Se aside and keep warm.

Omelet: In a small bowl, beat the eggs with the water or milk. In a small frying pan or omelet pan, melt 1 tablespoon butter over medium heat. Add the egg mixture, and cook the omelet, tilting the pan and carefully lifting the edges of the omelet in order to cook all of the egg without turning the omelet over. When omelet is cooked, add the vegetable and ham mixture on one side, fold the other side over, and place on the toasted bread. Salt and pepper the sandwich to taste and serve immediately. Yield: 1 sandwich.

Boston Baked Bean Sandwich

Baked beans were a staple of New England colonial kitchens. The early colonists learned how to cook dried beans from the Native Americans who traditionally baked their beans, flavored with maple sugar and bear fat, in deer hides placed in stone-lined pits.

New Englanders eventually substituted molasses and salt pork for the maple sugar and bear fat, creating what came to be known as Boston Baked Beans, which they also cooked slowly for many hours just as the Indians did. Molasses was a popular sweetener because of Boston's rum-producing role in the triangular trade of the day. Sugar cane grown in the West Indies was shipped to Boston and made first into molasses that was then used to make rum, a product that was used to buy slaves in West Africa for deployment in the West Indies cane fields.

Puritan housewives usually baked beans on Saturdays. This was because no cooking was permitted during the Sabbath, which lasted from sundown on Saturday through sundown on Sunday. The beans were eaten hot Saturday night and then served cold on Sunday.

Baked beans were typically served with brown bread, another food that evolved from the early New Englanders' dependence upon ingredients at hand. In those days, yeast wasn't available. Made from rye flour, cornmeal, molasses, and buttermilk, the unleavened brown bread was steamed, an English technique that held the colonists in good stead.

It is believed that the colonials were the first to combine brown bread and baked beans into a sandwich, and that the sandwiches quite possibly served as breakfast following Sabbath church services. This would indicate that the baked bean sandwich is quite possibly America's first and oldest sandwich.

It wasn't long before the popularity of baked beans spread far and wide. Wherever New Englanders migrated throughout the United States, they took with them their beloved receipts for baked beans and brown bread. By the time of the Civil War, Van Camp's Pork and Beans, a canned product introduced in 1861, were a popular staple in American homes. And by the late nineteenth century, baked beans were served in Boston restaurants where they were called "Boston Strawberries."

Baked bean sandwiches made their appearance in cookbooks published during the early twentieth century, including this one for "Cold Baked-Bean Sandwich, Club Style" in Janet Mckenzie Hill's 1909 edition of **Cooking for Two:**

Cold Baked-Bean Sandwich, Club Style

Butter two slices of Boston Brown Bread; on one of these dispose a heart leaf of lettuce holding one teaspoon of salad dressing; above the dressing set a generous tablespoon of cold, baked beans, then another lettuce leaf and dressing; finish with a second slice of bread, a tablespoon of beans, a floweret of cauliflower, and a teaspoonful of dressing over the cauliflower.

According to food writer Jean Anderson, baked beans still served a dual purpose during the 1930s. They were served on Friday night as a meatless dish and again, in the form of baked bean sandwiches, as the "Saturday night special." Baked beans were so popular during the 1930s that the Ferrara Pan Candy Company adopted the name "Boston Baked Beans" for sugar coated peanuts that were introduced in the early part of the

decade and which are still sold today.

Doubtless, baked bean sandwiches provided a nutritious, cost effective meal throughout the Depression as well as during the years of World War II rationing. During the war, all commercially canned baked beans were earmarked for the armed forces, so American cooks prepared baked beans from scratch.

By the 1950s, baked beans had become a favorite side dish served with barbecue. Boston, of course, is known as "Bean Town," and today, baked beans and baked bean sandwiches, often made with brown bread, are still a favorite Saturday night dinner throughout New England. And Americans everywhere celebrate July as National Baked Bean Month.

To the disappointment of many, Boston baked bean sandwiches have been dropped from today's trendy restaurant lunch menus. Fans will occasionally find them at small luncheonettes across the country where, in diner lingo, baked beans are called "whistle berries" or "Saturday nights."

Sandwich

Today's baked bean sandwich is likely to be a simple affair composed of cold, leftover baked beans piled between two slices of white bread. More often than not, the baked beans are prepared from one of several canned products sold in supermarkets. Garnishes typically include crispy slices of bacon, sliced onions, and/or ketchup.

Lobster Roll

There is as much controversy over where or
who developed the original lobster roll as there is
discussion over the proper preparation of this
pedigreed New England sandwich. Certainly, it is
a luxurious and tasty treat, containing plenty of
freshly cooked lobster. Once prevalent, and yet
disdained by early colonists who fed it to their
pigs, lobster today commands premium prices.

Very little information is available as to the
actual debut of the lobster roll. John Mariani says,
in **The Encyclopedia of American Food &
Drink**, that Harry Perry, owner of Perry's in
Milford, Connecticut, may have devised it in the
1920s. He adds that Perry supposedly had a sign
hanging up from 1927 until 1977 proclaiming his
establishment the "Home of the Famous Lobster
Roll." Jean Anderson points out that the lobster
roll is clearly a 20th century invention, and her
version in **The American Century Cookbook** is
based on the hamburger roll, which wasn't manufactured until 1912. As of this writing, the Maine
Lobster Promotion Council has resolved to inves-
tigate the matter further.

The popularity of the lobster roll is evident
throughout coastal New England where it can be
found in establishments ranging from posh restaurants to take-out seafood shacks. Lobster rolls also
take center stage at luncheons and suppers held
by churches and non-profit organizations, especially in Connecticut and Maine.

Tourists, familiar with Maine's famous lobsters,
equate lobster rolls with the perfect casual seaside meal along the state's coastline. Many flock
to the state in August when Lobster Month is
celebrated. Red's Eats in Wiscasset, Maine, has
been in business since 1938 and serves a lobster
roll par excellence - a whole lobster, with both
claw and tail meat, is served up in a buttered and
toasted bun. Owner Allen Gagnon has neatly
resolved the butter versus mayonnaise controversy by serving both on the side, and everyone
seems to be happy. In 1999, **Yankee Magazine**
picked Red's Eats as one of the most outstanding
reasons to visit Maine. Housed in a twenty-by-
eighteen foot seaside stand, Red's is strictly take-
out but provides a few picnic tables at which visitors can sit and enjoy those luxurious lobster rolls.

Sandwich

There are two very distinct camps of opinion
surrounding the correct preparation of a lobster
roll. In its purest form, chunks of fresh lobster are
gently laid into a buttered hot dog roll, melted
butter is poured lavishly over all, and the sandwich is served immediately. Contenders opt for
the lobster dressed with mayonnaise, celery, and
perhaps some kind of seasoning, such as lemon
juice and grated onion, spooned into a warm hot
dog bun. The latter is often topped with shredded
lettuce, an act that many classify as nothing short

of heresy. Most everyone agrees that the proper bun to use for a lobster roll is a hot dog bun that's cut on the top, rather than the sides, as it makes for easier loading.

Luscious Lobster Rolls

Perhaps the best way to savor pricey lobster is to avoid frills and keep it simple. Seafood shacks along the New England coast do a land office business catering to a public that adheres to this culinary rule.

2 large lobster tails
1 cup warm melted butter
4 quality hot dog or sausage rolls, top-cut if possible

Preheat grill and brush lightly with oil to keep lobster from sticking to grate. Remove lobster from shells, keeping the tails intact. Grill lobster tails over medium-high heat, brushing with melted butter, just until cooked through. Remove from grill and keep warm.

Preheat broiler and lightly toast the rolls. Cut each lobster tail in half lengthwise or chop the tail into half-inch pieces. Place a half tail or equivalent in each toasted bun and serve with remaining melted butter to drizzle over the lobster. Yield: 4 sandwiches.

Note: Whole lobsters, weighing about 1 pound, may be used. Plunge them into rapidly boiling water and cook 7 to 10 minutes. Drain, extract meat, and chop it into half-inch pieces. Lobster may be served warm or cold in lobster rolls.

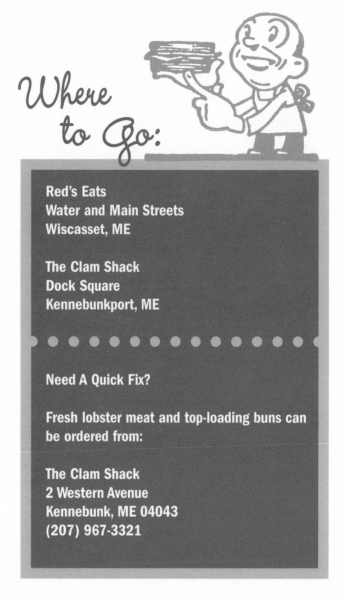

Where to Go:

Red's Eats
Water and Main Streets
Wiscasset, ME

The Clam Shack
Dock Square
Kennebunkport, ME

Need A Quick Fix?

Fresh lobster meat and top-loading buns can be ordered from:

The Clam Shack
2 Western Avenue
Kennebunk, ME 04043
(207) 967-3321

Cajun Shrimp-Stuffed Pistolette

Cajun stuffed pistolettes are virtually unknown outside of southern Louisiana. One might venture to say that they are Louisiana's best-kept secret. But what are they? First of all, one must understand that pistolettes are small, crusty, oval rolls, about 3 to 4 inches in length, similar to French rolls in taste and texture. Stuffed pistolettes contain ethereal mixtures of seafood combined with cheese, Cajun seasonings, and what, in Louisiana, is called "the trinity," because it appears in so many classic dishes: onions, celery, and bell peppers.

According to Franko Duet of Cut Off, Louisiana, stuffed pistolettes were created by the Cajuns sometime back in the 1920s. A frugal, hard-working people, the Cajuns didn't believe in letting anything go to waste. Day-old bread was put to especially good use. Early in the morning, before breakfast, Cajun housewives would fry the leftover pistolettes, hollow them out, and fill them with delicious mixtures of seafood. Wrapped tightly, the stuffed pistolettes were taken to work by Cajun fishermen. As one of America's first "fast food" sandwiches, they served as a delicious lunch later in the day.

Much of Louisiana's Cajun population has historically lived along Bayou Lafourche in Southeastern Louisiana. A former Mississippi river course, the bayou is paralleled by Highway 308, known as the "longest street in the world." It takes travelers south from Donaldsville in Ascension Parish, traversing nearly 100 miles along the length of Lafourche Parish, finally terminating at the Gulf of Mexico.

Stuffed pistolettes remained virtually unknown to tourists until Franko and Lois Duet introduced them, filled with crabmeat and shrimp, in their restaurants in Cut Off and Galliano, Louisiana, both located along the main artery of Bayou Lafourche. Savvy travelers in search of great Cajun bayou cooking were delighted with the pistolettes, and word soon spread of the delectable treat. It wasn't long before Frank Davis, host of **In the Kitchen with Frank Davis** on WWL TV in New Orleans, heard about those stuffed pisto-

lettes and invited Franko Duet to appear on his show. That event heralded the popularization of Cajun stuffed pistolettes throughout southern Louisiana where, today, they can be found at nearly every fair, festival, and community event. Although Franko and Lois closed their restaurants and retired, they continue to participate in many of these events where they can be found making their famous Cajun stuffed pistolettes.

Pistolettes are standard fare throughout most of Louisiana's Cajun country, including the Lake Charles area. Barry's Kitchen in Sunset, Louisiana, west of Baton Rouge, is known for homemade crawfish-stuffed pistolettes. Having operated their successful take-out shop for the past eleven years, Kitty and Frank Barry say they have all they can do to keep up with the demand for their pistolettes. At one time, their menu included other kinds of stuffed pistolettes, but due to the popularity of those containing crawfish, the rest were eliminated.

Sandwich

Cajun stuffed pistolettes, as mentioned above, are based on pistolette rolls that are plunged into hot oil and cooked for a minute or two on each side, creating a hot, crispy pocket that is typically filled with tasty seafood fillings like crab, crawfish, and shrimp. (It should be noted that some folks like to stuff their pistolettes before frying.) Chef Frank Davis has experimented with all sorts of combinations, and he says that a little creativity on the cook's part will result in stuffed pistolettes for breakfast, snacks, appetizers, dinner, and even dessert.

Frank's Cajun Shrimp-Stuffed Pistolettes

Reprinted with permission from Chef Frank Davis, whose most recent cookbook is *Frank Davis Cooks Cajun, Creole and Crescent City*, Pelican Publishing, Gretna, Louisiana.

2 sticks (1 cup) butter
2 cups finely chopped onions
¾ cup finely chopped celery
½ cup finely chopped red or green bell pepper
¼ cup finely sliced green onions
6 cloves garlic, finely minced
½ pound coarsely chopped mushrooms
3 cups evaporated milk
1 cup shrimp poaching stock (see notes)
1 pound Velveeta cheese, cut in chunks
5 pounds shrimp, poached and coarsely ground (see notes)
2 teaspoons Frank Davis Seafood Seasoning
1 teaspoon coarsely ground black pepper
½ teaspoon cayenne (red) pepper

½ gallon vegetable oil
24 unbaked pistolette

First, take a heavy 12-inch skillet and melt the butter over medium heat until it foams. Stir in onions, celery, bell pepper, green onions, garlic, and mushrooms, and cook them for about 12 to 15 minutes or until they are completely softened. Be careful not to let the butter burn!

When vegetables are cooked, pour in the evaporated milk and the poaching stock, mix thoroughly, and bring the mixture to a slow boil. Add all of the Velveeta chunks and, with the heat still set at medium, stir until the cheese melts and the sauce turns smooth and silky. This should take about 5 to 10 minutes. If it seems like there is a bit too much liquid, continue simmering, stirring frequently, until sauce is reduced a bit.

While the sauce is simmering, heat the vegetable oil to 350° in a high-sided frying pan or other deep pot.

Fold the ground shrimp into the hot sauce in the skillet, mix thoroughly, and cook the mixture for 3 minutes. Stir in the seafood seasoning, black pepper, and cayenne pepper. Remove pan from heat and allow the stuffing to cool slightly.

Drop the pistolettes into the hot oil, and fry them for a minute or two on both sides (kinda like doughnuts) until they turn a golden, crunchy brown. While pistolettes are still hot, hold them with a towel, make a slit in one end with a paring knife (big enough to insert a teaspoon), push down some of the bread with the knife on the inside of the pistolette to make a pocket, and fill the pocket with the stuffing.

While you can fill them all and keep them warm in a 200° oven for serving later, Cajun Shrimp-Stuffed Pistolettes are at their peak when served as they are made. Yield: 24 sandwiches.

Notes from Chef Frank:

To poach the shrimp, simmer them in water seasoned with crab boil and lemon juice just until they turn pink. Do not overcook them or they will turn gummy and rubbery.

If you want to make the stuffing spicy, substitute the Mexican-style jalapeño Velveeta for the regular Velveeta.

If you want to develop maximum flavor in the seafood mixture, make the stuffing a day before using it. Cover stuffing and place in the refrigerator overnight, and reheat it and stuff the pistolettes the next day. (But to be truthful, these are so good that'll probably never happen – you'll stuff the pistolettes as soon as you make 'em!) To serve the pistolettes at a party, go ahead and stuff them all at once. To seal the pistolettes so they don't leak, cut 6 pieces of American cheese in quarters and place a piece of cheese across the stuffing holes. The cheese will melt and seal the opening. Set pistolettes upright in muffin tins as they are made, keeping them warm in a 200° oven.

If you're thinking an injector or pastry bag might be an easy way to fill the pistolettes, forget it! You can't get enough stuffing into the center of the bread, and what you do get in ends up oozing back out because of the pressure created inside the bread.

Finally, experiment with different stuffings. Instead of shrimp, make the basic sauce but substitute sautéed crawfish, broiled oysters, Italian sausage and mozzarella cheese, smoked turkey, crabmeat, chopped chicken, or ham and bacon. The variations you can come up with are endless – but I guarantee you they'll all be delicious!

Note: If you cannot obtain pistolettes, packaged "brown and serve" Italian rolls, commonly available in supermarkets, may be substituted. Because they are smaller than pistolettes, you'll need a larger quantity.

Where to Go:

Souvlaki

Souvlaki (or souvlakia) is a traditional Greek dish that has been adopted and sometimes, adapted, by Greek immigrants and Americans into a popular sandwich. Many Greeks fleeing the Civil War in their homeland immigrated to the United States after World War II. They were followed by another influx when United States immigration laws were liberalized in 1965. The largest Greek community outside of Greece is in the Astoria section of Queens, New York, where many families established Greek shops and restaurants. One of the better-known Greek communities in the United States is in Tarpon Springs, Florida.

Sandwich

Normally made with pork in Greece, souvlaki in the United States is prepared in a number of ways. Sometimes, the meat (cuts of lamb, pork, or beef) is roasted on a large vertical rotisserie and the meat is then cut off in thin slices. Other times, small chunks of those same meats are placed on skewers called "souvla" and grilled. In both cases, the meat has been marinated in oil, lemon juice, oregano, and perhaps other herbs. The souvlaki sandwich is made by piling the meat into pita bread; lettuce, tomato, and feta cheese are added, and the whole is sauced with tzatziki.

Souvlaki

Marinade:
1 cup extra virgin olive oil
½ cup fresh lemon juice
5 cloves garlic, finely chopped
2 teaspoons dried oregano
1 teaspoon ground black pepper

3 pounds boneless pork, all fat removed, cut into 1-inch cubes

8 pocket-style pita bread rounds
Chopped red onion
Crumbled feta cheese
Iceberg lettuce, torn into small pieces
Chopped fresh tomato
Tzatziki (recipe follows)

Marinade: Whisk together all ingredients until well combined.

Mix cubed pork with marinade in a 13 x 9-inch glass baking dish, coating pork well. Cover and refrigerate for 24 hours to allow flavors to blend, turning meat at least once.

Preheat grill on medium high and brush grid lightly with olive oil to keep meat from sticking. Thread pork cubes on skewers, and discard marinade. Grill for 8 to 10 minutes, or until well browned and cooked through, turning frequently.

Meanwhile, preheat oven to 350°. Place pita bread on a baking sheet and heat through, about 5 minutes. Remove pita bread, cut each one in half, and open pockets. Remove pork from skewers, and fill each half pocket with some pork. Garnish with onion, feta cheese, lettuce, and tomato. Top with tzatziki and serve immediately. Yield: 8 whole sandwiches or 16 halves.

Tzatziki

2 cups plain yogurt
1 medium cucumber, peeled, seeded, grated, and well drained
2 cloves garlic, finely chopped
1 teaspoon dried dill weed
½ teaspoon salt
½ teaspoon ground white pepper
1 teaspoon extra virgin olive oil

Prepare tzatziki one hour before serving to allow flavors to blend. Combine all ingredients, mixing well. Cover and refrigerate. Yield: about 3 cups or enough for 8 whole souvlaki.

Where to Go:

Tony's Souvlaki (Opa, Opa)
28-44 31st Street
Queens, NY

Laikon Café
569 Monroe (Greektown)
Detroit, MI

Mr. Souvlaki
802 N. Pinellas Avenue
Tarpon Springs, FL

Falafel

Falafel is deliciously seasoned croquettes that are fried and served in pita bread. Popular throughout the Middle East, it's a typical street food in Israel where it's sold from pushcarts and sometimes referred to as the "Israeli hot dog."

Also known as *ta'amia*, falafel is made from dried white broad beans in Egypt while others make it with fava beans. In Israel, chick-peas (garbanzo beans) are used. A relative newcomer to the United States, it has become popular from coast to coast.

In California, San Jose's Falafel Drive-In has been in business since 1966 when the Nizbeh family established it. At the time, falafels were new to Americans, but the business grew along with the population explosion of San Jose and the Silicon Valley, and today, Falafel Drive-In, now a local landmark, may be one of the oldest purveyors of its namesake in the country.

Many enterprising Middle Eastern immigrants, of course, have helped introduce the falafel to America. Back in 1980, Moshe Mizarahi, newly arrived from Tel Aviv, decided to earn a living by doing what he knew best: making falafel, as his family had done in the Middle East for some 60 years. He set up a pushcart at the corner of Forty-sixth Street and Sixth Avenue in New York City's diamond district and gave away samples of his falafel. It wasn't long before Moshe had a booming business.

In Watertown, Massachusetts, Sepal is a Middle Eastern restaurant specializing in falafels. Owner Walid Massoud produces a version of the falafel that is wont to bring tears to the eyes of vegetarians on the prowl for a great meal.

Sandwich

In the United States, falafel is usually based on deep-fried balls made from ground chick-peas (garbanzo beans) that have been laced with herbs and spices, deep-fried, and stuffed into pita bread. While recipes vary widely, herb and spice selections include garlic, onion, parsley, mint, ground coriander, dried hot red peppers, black and cayenne peppers, sesame seeds, and/or salt. Sometimes, the chick-peas are also combined with fine bulgar or ground fava beans.

Toppings vary as well, including offerings like lettuce, tomatoes, onions, cucumber, and sweet pickles or pickled turnips. The latter are a Middle Eastern delicacy that even those who don't like turnips claim to be delicious. The sandwich is typically dressed with two sauces, a creamy tahini (sesame sauce), and a spicy-hot pepper and tomato sauce.

Falafel

½ **pound dried chick-peas, soaked overnight in cold water, drained, and rinsed**
2 **large cloves garlic, finely chopped**
1 **medium onion, finely chopped**
3 **tablespoons finely chopped Italian parsley**
3 **tablespoons finely chopped fresh cilantro**
½ **teaspoon salt**
½ **teaspoon ground black pepper**
½ **teaspoon ground cumin**
½ **teaspoon ground coriander**
¼ **teaspoon turmeric**
¼ **teaspoon cayenne pepper**
½ **teaspoon baking soda dissolved in ¼ cup cold water**

Vegetable oil for frying

6 **pocket-style pita breads**
Tahini (Sesame Sauce) (recipe follows)
Hot Sauce (recipe follows)
Chopped red onion
Iceberg lettuce torn into small pieces
Chopped fresh tomato
Chopped sweet pickles or gherkins
Pickled red turnip

In a large bowl, mix chick-peas with garlic, onion, parsley, cilantro, salt, pepper, cumin, coriander, turmeric, and cayenne. If the falafel balls will be made immediately, also add the baking soda dissolved in water at this time. If the falafel mixture is to be held in the refrigerator for more than a half hour, do not add the baking soda-water mixture until ready to use. Place half of mixture into a food processor fitted with a steel blade and process until it reaches the consistency of a smooth, but slightly gritty, paste. Remove paste to a bowl and repeat with remaining mixture. If holding mixture, cover with plastic wrap and refrigerate.

In a deep frying pan, add vegetable oil to a depth of one inch and heat to 375°. If necessary, add baking soda mixture to the falafel using an electric mixer. When oil is hot, shape falafel mixture into balls the size of large walnuts and drop into the oil, cooking up to eight balls at a time. Cook balls, turning to brown evenly, about 3 to 4 minutes. Remove with a slotted spoon and drain on paper towels. Keep warm until all falafel is cooked.

Meanwhile, preheat oven to 350° and heat pita bread for five minutes or just until warmed through. Remove and cut each pita in half. Place two falafel balls into each half and serve immediately with a choice of condiments. It's customary to put some of each condiment on the falafel along with both the tahini and hot sauces. Yield: 6 whole sandwiches or 12 halves.

Tahini (Sesame Sauce)

$1/2$ cup tahini paste, well stirred
$1/2$ cup lemon juice
$1/2$ cup water
2 cloves garlic, finely chopped
1 teaspoon salt
Pinch of cayenne pepper

In a medium bowl, whisk together all ingredients. Cover and set aside for at least one hour before serving to allow flavors to blend. Yield: About $1^1/2$ cups.

Hot Sauce

1 8-ounce can tomato sauce
1 2-ounce jar chopped red jalapeño peppers, undrained

$1/4$ teaspoon salt or to taste

In a small bowl, combine all ingredients and mix well. Cover and set aside for at least one hour before serving to allow flavors to blend. Yield: About 1 cup.

Where to Go:

Moshe's Falafel (pushcart)
Forty-sixth Street and Sixth Avenue
New York, NY

Falafel Drive-In
2301 Stevens Creek Boulevard
San Jose, CA

Sepal
17 Nichols Avenue
Watertown, MA

• • • • • • • • • • • • • •

Need A Quick Fix?

Order pickled turnip from:

Kalustyan's Food of Nations
123 Lexington Avenue
New York, NY 10016
Telephone: (212) 685-3451
Fax: (212) 683-8458
http://www.kalustyans.com

5

Today's
"Designer"
Sandwiches

Wraps

Wraps became trendy in the 1990s, creating a
new benchmark for the American sandwich.
According to Lori Lyn Narlock, co-author of
Wraps, they originated in San Francisco and
Northern California. The concept was based on
the enhancement and glamorization of the burri-
to, a long-established favorite throughout
California and the American Southwest. Usually
starting with a flour tortilla (but sometimes making use of flat bread), a variety of fillings are combined in imaginative pairings and laid on the tortilla, which is then folded in at one or both ends,
then rolled up from one edge of the tortilla.

Wraps were so well received in restaurants and
take-out shops that it wasn't long before they
spread across the country and began appearing in
airports and supermarket snack shops, offering yet
another alternative to the demand for "food-on-
the-run." While industry experts say the wrap
never really caught on in the Southwest and that
the wrap trend may have met its demise in
California, they continue to be popular throughout many parts of the country.

Sandwich

Plain white flour tortillas are the favored wrap,
but in many areas of the United States, flavored
tortillas, such as pesto and sun-dried tomato, are
in great demand because they add yet another
dimension of taste to these savory sandwiches.

As for the fillings and related condiments, they
run the gamut from traditional American to
international flavors and combinations, reflecting
the fact that many creators simply let their imagi-
nations run wild. In the international arena,
wraps often reflect the cuisine of Asia, Latin
America, and the Mediterranean. American
wraps are frequently based on chicken, turkey,
ham, or roast beef combined with some kind of
cheese that compliments the meat: fontina, provolone, blue, feta, Swiss, jack, mozzarella, and
American are among the favorites.

A variety of lettuces and other greens like fresh
spinach, basil, watercress, or cilantro provide
color, texture, and more taste. Wraps are further
dolled up with ingredients like thinly sliced
onion, roasted red peppers, crisp bacon, rice, hot
peppers, sun-dried tomatoes, black beans, avocado, and mushrooms.

Dressings add even more interest: plain old
mayo is flavored with ingredients like chiles,
pesto, lemon, lime, and tarragon, or it's replaced
by cream cheese or sour cream (flavored or plain),
Caesar dressing, ranch-style dressing, teriyaki, soy
or barbecue sauce, chutney, wasabi, guacamole,
and salsa – to name just a few.

Wraps are featured by a large variety of restaurants, take-out shops, and food vendors throughout the United States.

Sun-dried Tomato Wraps

Dressing:
1½ ounces dry packed sun-dried tomatoes
1 cup boiling water
1 cup mayonnaise
2 tablespoons Dijon-style mustard

¼ cup sour cream
2 tablespoons chopped fresh basil

4 10-inch sun-dried tomato-flavored flour tortillas
2 cups prepared mixed salad greens
¼ pound thinly sliced baked ham
¼ pound thinly sliced capicolla
¼ pound thinly sliced Genoa salami
8 thin slices provolone cheese

Dressing: Soak the sun-dried tomatoes in the boiling water for a half hour or until they are softened and pliable. Drain well and chop fine. To make dressing, combine chopped sun-dried tomatoes with mayonnaise, Dijon-style mustard, sour cream, and chopped basil. Refrigerate for at least one half hour prior to use to allow the flavors to blend.

Spread one quarter of the dressing on each of the four flour tortillas, covering the tortillas to within one inch of the edges. Sprinkle each with ½ cup salad greens. Divide the ham, capicolla, and salami among the four tortillas, layering in the order given. Top each with two slices of provolone cheese. Fold in the end of one side of each tortilla; then, beginning on one side, roll each tortilla until closed, leaving the other end open to showcase the filling. Yield: 4 wraps.

Gala Beef and Pepper Wraps

Dressing:
⅓ cup mayonnaise
⅓ cup Dijon-style mustard
3 tablespoons prepared horseradish

6 10-inch flour tortillas, plain or flavored
3 generous cups washed and trimmed fresh spinach
12 ounces thinly sliced roast beef

12 thin slices of Swiss cheese squares
1 12-ounce jar fire-roasted sweet red peppers, cut into thin strips

Dressing: Mix all ingredients for the dressing and refrigerate, covered, for at least one hour to allow flavors to blend.

Divide dressing (about 2 tablespoons each) among the six flour tortillas, spreading it to within one inch of the edges. On each tortilla, layer spinach, roast beef, Swiss cheese, and roasted red peppers. Fold in the end of one side of each tortilla; then, beginning on one side, roll each tortilla until closed, leaving the other end open to showcase the filling. Yield: 6 wraps.

Note: Substitute pocket pita bread for a delightful variation.

Panini

Panini, an Americanized Italian word that means "little bread," is actually a class of sandwiches in Italy, and it's the latest craze in the United States where sandwich fans continually prowl for new taste sensations. According to Fred Plotkin in **Italy Today: The Beautiful Cookbook**, they originated in Lombardy, where they are called "panino," in response to the demand among Milanese office workers for a quick lunch without sacrifice in flavor or quality. In recent years, Italians have enjoyed these grilled sandwiches filled with a seemingly endless and creative variety of fillings tucked into high quality bread. In both Italy and the United States, panini is eaten for lunch and as snacks and appetizers. In Italy, sandwich shops traditionally wrap the bottom of the *panino* in a crisp white paper napkin, providing a practical solution to drips while enhancing the aesthetics.

Panini is always grilled so most restaurants and café's have invested in professional grooved sandwich presses that flatten and heat the sandwich while creating a crunchy, buttery outer crust. Home cooks usually make do with two heated skillets: the sandwich is placed in the bottom pan and the top pan is lightly pressed down on the panini. Either way, the result is a whole new dimension added to the traditional concept of the American grilled cheese sandwich.

The creative potential of the panini was underscored in 2002 when, for the first time ever, a sandwich won the 40th Pillsbury Quick & Easy Bake-Off Cooking Contest. The winning recipe, worth a cool $1 Million, was Chicken Florentine Panini, made from refrigerated pizza dough, spinach, provolone cheese, and chicken breast. It's enough to make the old Earl of Sandwich blush with pride.

Sandwich

Quality Italian bread is an absolute must for a killer panini, and most sandwich chefs will opt for a relatively thin artisan bread like focaccia or ciabatta. The bread is sliced in half horizontally and cheese is laid on so that it melts during grilling. Next, the cheese is spread with some sort of dressing or condiment. The panini is then filled, but not overstuffed, with whatever strikes one's fancy. As with wraps, filling combinations tend to take on "themes" with the use of ingredients representative of specific cuisines such as Italian, French, or Mediterranean. Delicious panini vegetarian selections have garnered a large following even among meat eaters and often include grilled or roasted veggies.

Sun-dried Tomato and Salami Panini

For each sandwich:
**1 4 x 2-inch piece of focaccia, ciabatta,
or French bread**
Extra virgin olive oil
4 very thin slices of Genoa or hard salami
7 very thin slices of pepperoni
**1 generous teaspoon of finely julienned sun-dried
tomatoes packed in herbs and oil**
1 thin slice of provolone or mozzarella cheese

Be sure and have all ingredients at room temperature before making panini so the sandwich will warm properly and the bread won't burn. If using French bread, place the piece of bread on its side and slice off both the top and bottom layers to a thickness of about $1/2$ inch. Reserve interior bread slice for another use.

Lightly drizzle the inside of both the top and bottom slices of bread with olive oil. On the bottom slice of the bread, layer ingredients in the following order: salami, pepperoni, drained sundried tomatoes, and cheese. Cover sandwich with top of bread.

If you don't have a panini grill, a great substitute can be fashioned from a cast iron griddle and a cast iron frying pan. Place griddle on the stove and heat it over medium high heat. Place sandwich on the griddle and weight it down with the frying pan, pressing down lightly to compress the sandwich a bit. Fry the panini until the bread turns crispy and the filling is heated through, about 3 minutes per side. Remove from heat and serve immediately. Yield: 1 sandwich.

Where to Go:

Cafe Panini
2115 Allston Way
Berkeley, CA

Panini Garden
2715 Main Street
Santa Monica, CA

Eat Panini
2715 Main Street
Los Angeles, CA

Stuffed Pita Bread Sandwiches

Pita bread, introduced by Middle Eastern immigrants to the United States, was traditionally used for ethnic specialties like falafel and souvlaki. Today, it has become a mainstream element in our sandwich cuisine, and pita bread is used by chefs, vendors, and home cooks alike as the basis for creative sandwiches that include all manner of delicious fillings. Here are a couple of examples of pita-based sandwiches to stimulate your imagination.

Grilled Chicken and Blue Cheese Pitas
Reprinted with permission from Chef Robbie Mayerat, Rushford Lake, NY.

Dressing:
1 cup finely chopped red onion
$3/4$ cup finely chopped celery
$1/2$ cup finely chopped red bell pepper
$1/2$ cup finely chopped orange bell pepper
$1^{1}/_{2}$ cups mayonnaise
1 cup sour cream
$1^{1}/_{2}$ teaspoons garlic powder
$1^{1}/_{2}$ teaspoons dried oregano
1 8-ounce package blue cheese, crumbled

3 whole chicken breasts (about $2^{1}/_{2}$ pounds)
1 teaspoon salt
1 teaspoon pepper
12 pocket-style pita breads (white or whole wheat)
Lettuce for garnish

Dressing: In a large bowl, combine onion, celery, peppers, mayonnaise, sour cream, garlic powder, oregano, and blue cheese. Mix well, cover, and refrigerate.

Preheat outdoor grill or broiler. Salt and pepper chicken breasts and grill until completely cooked through and golden on all sides. Remove from grill and cut chicken into $1/2$ inch pieces. You should have about 5 cups of chicken. While still slightly warm, combine chicken with dressing so the blue cheese softens a bit. Cover and refrigerate.

Preheat oven to 350°. Place pita rounds on baking sheets and heat in oven just until warmed through. Cut each pita in half, open into pockets, and stuff with about $1/2$ cup filling. If desired, tuck a bit of lettuce on each side of the filling. Serve immediately. Yield: 12 whole sandwiches or 24 half sandwiches.

Note: Substitute mini pita pockets to make hearty cocktail sandwiches or snacks. You'll need about 2 dozen mini pita rounds.

Ranch Pita Pocket

Vegetable or canola oil
$2^1/_2$ pounds of $^1/_4$-inch thick top round steak, cut in 1 x $^1/_2$ inch strips

8 pita pocket breads, white or whole wheat
10 ounces crumbled feta cheese
1 small red onion, chopped
2 cups chopped lettuce
4 medium fresh tomatoes, cut in small chunks
Ranch salad dressing and/or Italian salad dressing

Heat a wok or medium-sized frying pan and add 1 tablespoon vegetable or canola oil. Heat oil until it just begins to smoke, and add a handful of the beef strips. Stir-fry about 3 minutes over high heat until just cooked through and browned; remove to a paper towel-lined platter to drain. Repeat procedure for remaining beef, adding 1 tablespoon oil for each batch and being careful not to add too much beef at a time or it will not brown.

Meanwhile, preheat oven to 350°. Place pitas in oven for about for 5 minutes or until just heated through. Cut pitas in half, open pockets slightly, and divide beef among them.

Serve with feta cheese, red onion, lettuce, and tomato placed in small serving bowls so that each person can prepare pitas to individual taste. Top pitas with Ranch dressing or Italian salad dressing. Yield: 8 whole sandwiches or 16 halves.

6

The Future

The Shelf-Stable Sandwich

America's men and women in the armed forces are in for a treat beginning in 2004. A new pocket sandwich will be included in their "Meal, Ready-to-Eat" (MRE) battlefield rations. MREs historically contained ingredients, separately packaged in pouches, from which soldiers could make their own sandwiches. The problem was that sandwiches couldn't be prepared in advance, because the bread would turn soggy from moisture in the other ingredients. Now, food technicians at the United States Army Soldier Systems Center in Natick, Massachusetts, have devised a method that literally locks the moisture into foods like barbecued chicken and pepperoni. As a result, they are taking the all-American sandwich in a new direction.

Substances called humectants are added so there's no danger of water leakage and these additives also limit bacterial growth. The result is a sandwich, sealed in a laminated plastic pouch, which can be eaten on the move, that survives rough handling and extreme climates, and that will stay fresh for up to three years at 26° C. The lab folks refer to it as the "shelf-stable sandwich."

Current offerings of the pocket-type sandwiches include barbecued chicken and the pepperoni pocket. Other additions to the menu will include peanut butter sandwiches, pocket pizzas, breakfast burritos, and cream cheese-filled bagels.

The military was responsible for the development or promotion of products that, today, are commonly found in American supermarkets, including processed cheese, dehydrated eggs, and freeze-dried coffee. Who knows? Perhaps the new long-life sandwich will be available from our local grocers in the not too distant future. As for marketing of the product, we can probably expect some savvy advertiser to promote it as the perfect solution to unexpected dinner guests!

shooting
sandwiches

*or, How We Put Together
A Special like
"Sandwiches That You Will Like"
By Rick Sebak*

I have been really lucky, getting to make TV programs
for PBS about some of the best parts of American
culture (hot dogs, beaches, ice cream, amusement parks
and flea markets), but this project about great American
sandwiches was one of the very best experiences
of them all. There are few rules in producing a video
documentary, and I think I've forgotten what they are
anyway, but I find that people are always
interested in the process. So I kept a diary
in my laptop. Here are some of the entries:

*sandwich
crew*

Monday December 17 2001
WQED Pittsburgh

We start fast. I'm in the midst of shooting a new local documentary about the winter holidays in Pittsburgh, when I get about a week to whup together a proposal for a new national program about sandwiches across the country, sort of a follow-up to *A Hot Dog Program* that we made back in 1999. The fund-raising folks at PBS want a show that will entertain and inspire people to contribute to their public television stations, and I think sandwiches will be a perfect topic. Truth is: I've been thinking about this idea for years and saved a little piece of clip art that I found once on the inside of an old matchbook. It has three views of a little guy eating a sandwich and it says, *Sandwiches That You Will Like*. A good title.

I finish putting my ideas on paper today, and send the proposal off to PBS.

Wednesday February 13 2002
WQED Pittsburgh

Today in the hall on the third floor, I find out that PBS's fund-raising folks have said "Yes" to the SANDWICHES proposal. The program has to be shot and edited by October 1 for a December airdate. We've budgeted 18 days of shooting and 12 travel days with 10 weeks of editing to get it all into shape. We'll see what we can do.

Friday May 31 2002
Pittsburgh to Cuba

After a couple of months of sporadic research and planning while editing that local holidays show, I get together with the whole *Sandwiches* field crew today for the first time. We're going on our first "shooting" trip: a swing through the northeast. I'm ready and eager, bolstered by my fortune cookie message from lunch yesterday: "You are about to start a delightful journey."

Traveling with me will be the trusty Bob Lubomski, sound engineer, chief vehicle packer and all around wizard on this project; Minette Seate, my amicable associate producer, responsible for everything from setting up stories to nitty-gritty stuff: videotapes, releases, vehicle and motel reservations, flyers that we will hand out to curious people at the various locations, and snacks; Jarrett Buba, an energetic freelance lighting guy who worked on the holidays program; and Buck Brinson, my old buddy and cameraman (or "director of photography" as he likes to call himself) who lives now in Hollywood, Florida. He and I first worked together in South Carolina in the early 1980s, and in recent years, we have found ways to work together again.

So, we pick up Buck at the Pittsburgh airport, load him into our big white whale of a rented Ford van, and hit the highway north to New York state, swaying in the wind, and stopping this first night in Cuba, a beautiful little town with some tasty local cheeses. We love the fact that our rooms are really cheap ($45 a night).

Saturday June 1 2002
Cuba to Rushford Lake to West Seneca

Our first shoot is not far from Cuba, at the home of Becky Mercuri, the food author who's agreed to write a companion book for our show. She and I "met" when she sent an e-mail message to our HOT DOG site, and we've exchanged so many messages that I feel I know her before we ever meet face to face. Full of energy and enthusiasm, she's helped with research and story ideas, and I've tried to squelch her fears about this on-camera stuff. We interview her in her big, beautiful kitchen, asking about the history of sandwiches and the local specialty, beef-on-weck.

Then, we all drive toward Buffalo, to West Seneca, New York, where Schwabl's, a classy little restaurant, sells legendary beef-on-weck sandwiches. It's old and wonderful beyond my wildest expectations. We shoot from just after lunchtime until well into the dinnertime rush when I think the Schwabl's folks start getting a little tired of our lights and cables and bulky camera-and-tripod always in the way.

Before dark, we head for our Buffalo motel, happy: it is a good first day of shooting.

Sunday June 2 2002
Buffalo to Natick

We're on the road all day, Western New York to Eastern Massachusetts.

For dinner in Natick, just west of Boston, we get Chinese delivered to Jarrett's room at the Travelodge so we can all watch the season finale of *Six Feet Under*.

Monday June 3 2002
Natick to Watertown to Revere

At the gate into the U.S. Army's Soldiers System Center, we find out that the registration on our rental van has expired. It actually expired the day we picked up the van. Security here is post-nine-eleven strict, but they let us enter with warnings about fines and possible future stops.

We're here to check out the Combat Feeding Program, to see the "shelf-stable sandwich," a newfangled, super-military-meal that lasts up to three years in its package (with no refrigeration!) It's a slow day around the lab, but we get some fun interviews on tape, shoot some ongoing experiments, and Patty Welsh, the media liaison, promises to get us some footage the next time they crank up the sandwich-making machinery.

We decide to have lunch at our next location, Sepal, a Middle Eastern restaurant in nearby Watertown, Massachusetts, and we are surprised by a magnificent

midday feast, compliments of Walid Massoud, our next subject. A Palestinian immigrant who came to study in Boston in the 1970s, Walid fries and bakes the best falafel I've ever tasted, and we are all won over by his charm, his excellent cooking, his loyal customers, and his theories about peace-making through food. We hang around for dinner (some of the luncheon leftovers brilliantly embellished) and consider staying here forever.

Tuesday June 4 2002
Revere to Portland

It's a beautiful day at Revere Beach on Boston's North Shore. Brian McCarthy and the folks at Kelly's Roast Beef are generous, accommodating, funny, and the food is dynamite. I think the clam chowder is remarkably good, and we love the fact that people take sides on the seafood-or-roast-beef issue. We get a good mix of customers and love the Boston brogue in so many of the voices.

We finish our shooting and eating by mid-afternoon and hit the road north to Maine. Minette has made reservations in Portland.

Wednesday June 5 2002
Portland to Wiscasset to Portland

Raining at dawn, it's just gray, cool and overcast by the time we get to Wiscasset, about fifty miles north of Portland. Red's is a little red shack beside U.S. Highway 1, under a huge tree, just a stone's throw from the Sheepscot River. I'm worried about all the attention this place has already received on TV, in books, magazines and websites, but Al Gagnon and his daughter, Debbie Cronk, are totally accommodating and enthusiastic about our being there. And their lobster

rolls are so simple and sublime that I know I will crave them forever.

Midmorning, we meet Holly Moore too. I've been on his website, www.hollyeats.com, about a thousand times, and we've talked on the phone, but here's our first encounter, and he gives us a sharp, expert interview with a dry sense of humor.

Today is also my forty-ninth birthday, and our lobster lunch here is what I'll remember most. Great food, lively interviews, no technical problems, everything an aging TV producer could hope for.

Thursday June 6 2002
Portland to Sandwich to Tarrytown

A gray and drizzly travel day. We head south out of Maine, heading for Cape Cod. Originally for this project I hoped to get to Hawaii (once called the Sandwich Islands, named for the same Earl of Sandwich who gave a name to meat between bread), but that now seems unlikely, so we settle instead for a short side trip to Sandwich, Massachusetts. Minette found a website for the Earl of Sandwich Motel here, and we laugh at all the Sandwich stuff, from the Sandwich Police to a shop called Sandwich's Sandwiches.

After lunch, somewhere in Connecticut, it starts to rain again. After dark, Jarrett drives us through a horrific rain storm as we enter New York. I-95 is narrow and very scary here. Too many huge trucks. Everyone is going too fast, too close together, it's too dark, too dangerous, and we're tired. We are relieved to be alive when we get to the Marriott Courtyard in Tarrytown, a place we stayed before, when we were making *A Flea Market Documentary* in 2000.

Friday June 7 2002
Tarrytown to Manhattan, Lower East Side

Driving a big van into New York City, we worry. Where will we park? Will our equipment be safe? Will we find a parking lot near Katz's Deli where we're supposed to spend the day? All pointless worrying. We find an empty meter right on Houston Street in front of Katz's, and we get all our equipment inside long before lunchtime madness begins.

The owner, Alan Dell, is a sassy interview, but so are lots of New Yorkers -- good, loquacious, opinionated people. The food is stupendous, and I love any place that makes its own mustard and its own pickles.

Buck and Bob squeeze in behind the counter to see and hear how the countermen work, watching their speedy knives, listening to their exchanges with the customers. As he often does, Bob starts interviewing people too and says he's gotten some great responses.

Saturday June 8
Tarrytown to Greenwich Village to Harrisburg

We're back in the city before 9:00 am on Saturday morning. It's been a bit of a hassle setting up this shoot at Peanut Butter & Company. Lee Zelban, the young man who founded this place, has had so many TV crews here that he isn't excited about more attention. The whole scene is a bit odd and uncomfortable.

But the customers are great: a good mix of tourists, smart alecks and other first-timers, and we're knocked out by two young girls named Jemma and Emily who are bright and giggly and fun, and when Jemma launches into an unsolicited history of the Earl of Sandwich, we're really in love. Before they get away, we ask the girls to do an on-camera promo for us, a little commercial for the show, and they are instantly professionals.

By mid-afternoon, we're back in the big Ford van, heading home but stopping overnight in Harrisburg.

Sunday June 9 2002
Harrisburg to Pittsburgh

We get home with plenty of time to get Buck to

the airport for his five o'clock flight to Florida. As my cookie predicted, it has been a delightful journey. I can only hope the rest of our travels will be so successful.

Monday, June 10 2002
WQED Pittsburgh

Kevin Conrad, my friend and editor, has been working on the Pittsburgh holidays program while we've been gone. Now he'll start thinking about *Sandwiches*. He and I have worked together since my first show at WQED in 1987, and I don't have to worry about him doing anything but great work.

In the evenings, our assistant editor, Matt Conrad (no relation to Kevin although we kid them both about being brothers, cousins and even father-and-son sometimes) will take the tapes we shot on our trip and he'll "digitize" them into our computer so Kevin and I can work with the footage, using the nonlinear editing system called Avid. Matt is bringing on an intern, Stacie Martin, a student from Pittsburgh Filmmakers.

Sunday June 23 2002
San Francisco

At a reception today, part of the PBS Annual Meeting, I run into Gustavo Sagastume, the PBS Vice President who's in charge of fundraising among other things. He says my program has been chosen to be a TOOP, a Target of Opportunity Outside Pledge. This means that it will air nationally in February, not in a pledge period, but as a special pledge "event" in the regular PBS program schedule. Cool. These TOOPs are a relatively new idea, and I like it. It also means we might get an extended deadline.

Friday July 5 2002
Pittsburgh to Philadelphia

The Fourth of July is busy in Philadelphia, but I figure all those tourists are gonna want a cheese steak at some point, so we make a quick weekend trip across Pennsylvania. Minette has other plans, so we're a small crew, working this time with another one of my cameraman buddies, Steve Willing, who works for

KDKA-TV2 here in Pittsburgh.

I've never been to either of the two most famous cheese steak places, Pat's or Geno's, but I love the way everyone takes sides about which is better. I know right away I'm definitely a Pat's guy, but Holly Moore, who's our guide to Philadelphia, likes Geno's better, so we seriously try to capture both sides of the issue.

Saturday July 6 2002
Philadelphia

Ah, Saturday morning in the Italian Market! At George's Sandwich Shop (a place Holly suggested that I thought would be just a mention in the show), the owner, Mark Onorato, shows us his grandfather's old calling card with our *Sandwiches That You Will Like* clip-art logo on it! We stay and shoot there most of the morning. Mark's daughter, Audrey, is fun because she takes our interview so seriously.

Then, we spend a couple of hours at another Holly Moore favorite, Chickie's Italian Deli, where Jean and Henry George make some world-class hoagies, including a really tasty Veggie hoagie.

We've got plenty of Philadelphia material, but Holly leads us out to the Roxborough neighborhood to taste the cheesesteak at Dalessandro's. We all agree it's the best we've tasted so far. Philly is full of surprises.

Sunday July 7 2002
Philadelphia to Pittsburgh

Homeward bound, we get off the PA Turnpike for lunch at Zinn's Diner and a brief stop nearby at Renninger's Antique Market.

Monday July 8 2002
WQED Pittsburgh

Kevin and I really start to edit this stuff. We have to work fast to meet all our deadlines, and I've got a Midwest trip to set up too.

Friday July 12 2002
Pittsburgh to Chicago

Minette has to have some minor surgery, so she's staying home, but Bob and Jarrett and I spend the morning trying to find a rental van that we like, then we head off across Ohio.

When we get to the Chicago airport that evening to pick up Buck, he's not there. I call his cell phone and find out that because of bad Florida weather, he missed a connecting flight, and he's stuck in Atlanta overnight with reservations on the first flight to Chicago early tomorrow.

Saturday July 13 2002
Chicago

Buck is waiting curbside when we get to O'Hare at 8:00 a.m., and we head directly into the city, to Mr. Beef on Orleans. Dominic Zuccharo, who runs this place with his brother Joe, isn't surprised to see us but says he wasn't sure if today was the day or not. Pat Bruno, food writer and critic, has set this all up, and he arrives moments later. We spend some time in the kitchen, sample some sausage, grab a dozen or so really enthusiastic interviews, and finally taste these fabled Italian beef sandwiches topped with homemade giardiniera. I find that I like them better than Philly cheese steaks; they're juicy and soft, spicy and crunchy all at once.

In the afternoon, Pat leads us to Buona Beef in Hillside, where we meet Joe Buonavolanto, taste some

suburban-style sandwiches there, and we finish the day full of beef. I first learned to love Chicago when we were here for *A Hot Dog Program*, and Italian beef just increases my affection.

Sunday July 14 2002
Chicago to Marshalltown

There's a lot of corn growing on both sides of the highway as we head into Iowa. Around Bettendorf, I realize we can get off I-80, go north and hop on the Lincoln Highway for part of the drive. It's truly the great American highway that so many people think Route 66 was.

Unexpectedly, we find a really good Mexican dinner in Marshalltown.

Monday July 15 2002
Marshalltown

When I'm paying for our rooms in the motel lobby, I meet Floyd Buffington, a retired truck driver, who asks what we're doing and says, "PBS television? You know what my favorite PBS show is? The one I saw about diners in Pennsylvania." I like this guy instantly because I made that program back in 1993, and when he says he used to work at Taylor's Maid Rite, I invite him to meet us there.

"Maid Rites" are simply cooked, ground beef sandwiches, an Iowa tradition of sorts, like a sloppy joe with no sauce, and all the people we meet at Taylor's Maid Rite know them and love them, and their affection is contagious. The restaurant (with stools around a big U-shaped counter) is classic. The owner, Don Taylor Short, understands the place's importance to the community, and the fact that they butcher the beef downstairs is unexpected and amazing. And you've got to respect the practicality of getting a sandwich with a spoon. I love this story, too.

We interview many people, including Floyd. By mid-afternoon, we wander back onto the highway and go as far as Burlington, Iowa, before we find a place to stay for the night.

Tuesday July 16 2002
Burlington to St Louis

I'm apprehensive about St Louis because I haven't been able to set up a place where we can watch how a St Paul sandwich (egg foo yung on white bread) is made. I found an excellent on-line article about St Pauls written by a young St Louis writer named Thomas Crone who's going to help us. He doesn't seem worried about our lack of location. "We'll find a place," he says.

Buck, Bob and Jarrett are relaxing at the motel pool while I continue to make calls. St Louis is known for lots of unusual sandwiches, and I'm thinking we ought to check out a few, maybe even tonight.

Before dinner, we meet Thomas, and his friend Kurt Gretsch, and we go to North County to try some of the sandwiches at Daryle Brantley's C&K Barbecue. He's got snoots (baked pig noses), ears (wobbly, boiled flaps of pork cartilage) and some excellent rib tips that he tops with a splendiferous sauce, a scoop of potato salad and Wonder bread. It's a fascinating place, but just a quick stop because I know this will be merely a mention (not a story) in the program.

Wednesday July 17 2002
St Louis

Based on their earlier travels together in search of good St Paul sandwiches, Thomas and Kurt suggest we first try a place called Kim Van on Gravois in the Fox Park neighborhood. They remember it as colorful with big booths, and when I go in and ask Jennifer Nguyen if we can come in with our camera and shoot some TV, she says Yes. It's amazing that some people can be so cooperative and adventurous.

Buck tapes Jennifer making the sandwiches, we interview Thomas and Kurt, and we take over more than half of the front of the restaurant, rearranging the booths, setting up lights and trying to leave space for real customers. Jennifer and her husband, Island, are Vietnamese, and with their two young daughters, they seem amused by all our silly work. They reward us with a huge lunch, including samples of some of their best dishes, when all we really needed was a few St Pauls.

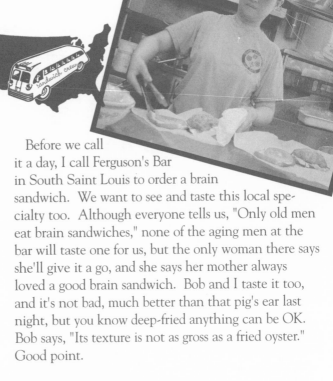

Before we call it a day, I call Ferguson's Bar in South Saint Louis to order a brain sandwich. We want to see and taste this local specialty too. Although everyone tells us, "Only old men eat brain sandwiches," none of the aging men at the bar will taste one for us, but the only woman there says she'll give it a go, and she says her mother always loved a good brain sandwich. Bob and I taste it too, and it's not bad, much better than that pig's ear last night, but you know deep-fried anything can be OK. Bob says, "Its texture is not as gross as a fried oyster." Good point.

Thursday July 18 2002
St Louis to Louisville

We spend most of the day in the van. We stumble onto a cheap lunch in a tiny town in Indiana and then a big dinner at a restaurant called Z near our motel in Louisville. On the road, eating is often an adventure, full of surprises, and our only rule is to avoid chain restaurants.

Friday July 19 2002
Louisville to Jeffersonville

The Brown Hotel is probably the fanciest place we are including in this show, but the Hot Brown sandwich is such a perfect subject for us that we can't pass it up. A friend at the Corporation for Public Broadcasting had told me to be sure to check out this Louisville classic. Then while researching the Hot Brown, I realized it's very close to what we in Pittsburgh would call a "Devonshire" sandwich: open-faced turkey topped with a melted cheese sauce, tomato and bacon.

The executive chef at the hotel, Joe Castro, does quite a bit of TV for one of the local stations in Louisville, and he's ready to start when we get to the

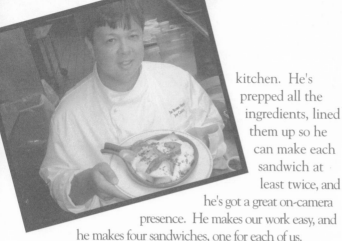

kitchen. He's prepped all the ingredients, lined them up so he can make each sandwich at least twice, and he's got a great on-camera presence. He makes our work easy, and he makes four sandwiches, one for each of us.

Then we go down to the restaurant at the front of the hotel, interview some employees and a few customers there. Buck also grabs shots of the beautiful old black-and-white photos hanging on the restaurant's walls.

About 4:00 p.m., we leave Buck with the hotel's bellman, knowing that he can catch the next shuttle to the Louisville airport, while Bob, Jarrett and I take the van onto Interstate 71 toward Cincinatti, heading for home. We find some cheap rooms at Jeffersonville, Ohio, right next to an outlet mall where we end the day with some bargain shopping. New shoes.

Saturday July 20 2002
Jeffersonville to Pittsburgh

At lunchtime, we stop in Wheeling at Coleman's Fish Market for the famous fish sandwich which Jane and Michael Stern have written about in *Roadfood* and *Gourmet* magazine. Of course, we all think we know of several better fish sandwiches in Pittsburgh, but Coleman's is a really good, unusual fresh fish market with an odd ordering system (always a sign of good food, I think).

It's not far from Wheeling to Pittsburgh, and we're home, unpacked, with the van returned before dinnertime.

Friday July 26 2002
Pittsburgh

I could easily make an hour-long program about just Pittsburgh sandwiches. This is a great sandwich city, and I'm hoping I'll get to mention several in the show. We spend most of our day at the Isaly's dairy store in

West View, talking to Tom and Gail Weisbecker about their excellent sandwiches, especially the Slammer, a half-pound of grilled chipped ham (a beloved Pittsburgh foodstuff) with cheese and fried onions on a homemade bun. Over the past year or two, I've learned to love this place, these people and the whole scene, and I'm really happy they have agreed to be part of the show.

Interviewing people you know, however, is different than asking questions to strangers. Tom and Gail both want to respond with quick, smart-alecky answers, and I want them to be garrulous.

Steve Willing is the cameraman again today, and Paul Ruggieri, one of our staff at WQED, is running audio because Bob had another freelance job today that paid more. Jarrett is here, however, setting and moving lights, helpful in a million ways as always. And Minnette makes sure we don't dawdle.

When we're done at Isaly's, we also swing by Charlie's in North Oakland (where Chuck Wallander makes the best cheesesteaks at this end of Pennsylvania), shoot a quick interview and a sandwich being made, then on to Chiodo's Tavern in Homestead (where Joe Chiodo and his crew make the incredible "Mystery Sandwich" with a secret set of ingredients.) I fear I'm shooting too much material.

Thursday August 8 2002
Pittsburgh to New Orleans

Minette has made all our plans to fly to New Orleans on US Airways, found us a place to stay not far from the French Quarter, and arranged for the rental of a van while we're here. Buck is already there when we arrive. We get into town, go to a place called Mother's for a huge New Orleans lunch, and we spend the rest of the afternoon and evening wandering around.

Friday August 9 2002
New Orleans

Picking a place for a certain kind of sandwich is sometimes a challenge. Minette and I agonized, conferred and researched about where we might find really good seafood po-boy sandwiches in this city that made them famous. Uglesich's sounded good (but it's closed all summer), the Louisiana Seafood Exchange in Jefferson had some new name (Crabby Jack's) that sounded silly, the French Quarter places seemed too touristy, and so we thought this Domilise's place seemed promising. We lucked out. The carefully constructed sandwiches, the women who make them, the easy going local dialect, the many Uptown regulars who eat there, and the Barq's root beer in a bottle made it a truly memorable experience. You can eat phenomenally well in this Crescent City.

Saturday August 10 2002
New Orleans

We get to Central Grocery in the French Quarter early. Larry Tusa, who worked with Minette to coordinate our visit, has suggested that we do all interviews in the morning before the crowds arrive, although folks are already munching on muffulettas when we get there at 9:00 a.m. (I had been to New Orleans only once before, back in the 1980s, and I was alone then, and oddly, all I got to eat that trip was one of these unusual round, cold cut-and-olive-salad sandwiches at Central Grocery because it had been recommended by a friend.) The store itself is a classic little Italian groceria, crammed full of imported specialties, and we take up too much room with all of our equipment, but Larry is energetic, his brother Frank is frank, and behind the counter, Viola Jones gives a slightly goofy tour of the ingredients and introduces her co-workers. Buck gets up on a ladder to get some high-angle shots. We grab as many images as we can, talk to as many people as there's time for, and hope we don't adversely affect today's business. That's what we always try to do no matter where we go.

Sunday August 11 2002
New Orleans to Houston

Today is gravy. It's an easy travel day. Larry Tusa gave us a couple of muffulettas to take with us, assuring us that they would be excellent if eaten within forty-eight hours. We get to our motel in Houston, check in, then sit in the breakfast area and split the day-old sandwiches. They are still scrumptious, maybe even better than the fresh ones we sampled yesterday.

Later, Bob, Jarrett, Buck and I sit poolside at the motel and play some cards, making us miss the agreed upon time for dinner, and Minette is not happy with us, but the Tex Mex feast we find at a nearby restaurant makes everything OK, the best fajitas we ever tasted.

Monday August 12 2002
Houston

About a month ago, Minette set up a shoot at a barbecue place in Houston, but the owners backed out about a week ago, saying they were having some remodeling done, and didn't want any TV attention right now. Ugh. So, we had to find another place in Houston. A search on Google.com led us to a newspaper article that led us to a place called Thelma's in the Third Ward. We are very lucky again. When you meet someone like Thelma Williams, you know you've met a force of nature, and when she's cooking some juicy, wonderful-smelling meat, you have to acknowledge that sometimes things do work out for the best. We have an unforgettable day in Thelma's modest little house in a dismal, flat, warehouse-y sort of neighborhood, where she dishes out stupendous food on a daily basis. This is certainly the best beef barbecue I've ever tasted. The sauce is spicy, sweet, unique. The warm, homey, unpretentious and upbeat atmosphere

is even better. The sandwiches aren't "liftable" because they're swimming in the sauce. It doesn't matter. The chicken sandwiches and the rib ones are full of bones anyway. Who cares when the stuff is so delicious! The clientele is just as enthusiastic about the place as we are.

When Buck finally says that he thinks we may have enough "stuff" to put together a story, we break for a late lunch. There are a lot of sandwiches (including the four catfish ones that Buck ordered in the kitchen) to taste and devour, and Thelma puts together a big sampler platter of her side dishes too.

Minette and Thelma's granddaughter, Keirra, hit it off big time, and they hang out as we wrap up the festivities and the equipment. We are sorry that such days have to end.

Tuesday August 13 2002
Houston to Pittsburgh

Bob wants to stay till Thelma's opens today so he can get a whole brisket to take home, but we've got to be at the airport by 9:30 a.m., so we leave Texas with no extra beef. We know where to get a great sandwich in Houston however.

Matt picks us up at the airport in Pittsburgh, and then he and Stacie will spend most of the evening loading and "logging" these fresh new tapes of po-boys, muffulettas and barbecue sandwiches into the computer.

Wednesday August 14 - Friday August 16

These are frantic days filled with trying to set up sandwich locations in California, editing some of the earlier stuff, and wondering if we can get this all done.

Saturday August 17 2002
Pittsburgh to San Jose, California

I've tried several different avenues, but nothing has led me to the right place for *banh mi*, the Vietnamese sandwiches that I've learned to love. Most histories of these things points to San Jose as the American "point of entry," and there's a big Vietnamese population here, so we thought this was the best place to find a good example of these cilantro-carrot-and-other-stuff-laden treats on French bread.

Once we check into our motel, Minette and Buck and I go "scouting," looking for a cooperative sandwich shop. I've made a list of businesses and addresses, and we try our first *banh mi* in downtown San Jose at a tiny little place with lots of sandwiches to choose from. We like the *banh mi* on homemade bread, but we doubt we could get our camera in there and leave room for customers, so we eat and drive on.

Heading south to check out one place that's written up several places on the internet, we pass a strip-style shopping center, and Minette says "Look! There's a sandwich place!" So I turn in to check out Huong Lan Sandwiches. It's immediately a good possibility because there are lots of people there, exotic pieces of meat are hanging on hooks in a sort of deli department on the left as you walk in, and the place is full of activity. And there's a big, well-lit, suspended menu that tells you what types of sandwiches are available. We ask to speak to the manager, explain what we want to do, and he hesitates only a moment before saying, "OK, but I won't be here tomorrow, my brother-in-law will be, but he speaks better than me anyway. Ask for Patrick when you get here tomorrow."

We have a location, and it looks good.

Sunday August 18 2002
San Jose to Los Angeles, California

When we get to Huong Lan about 9:30 a.m., Patrick Lam is expecting us, but he hopes we will be gone in an hour or so. I tell him we'll probably take more time than that, and he smiles uncomfortably, so we get to work. As usual, Buck says he will start by shooting a few "exteriors" of the place. When he gets the camera on the tripod and puts a tape in, he realizes something is wrong. The tape deck won't "engage." Buck and Bob and Jarrett start looking at the various things that might be wrong that they might know how to fix. I start making calls. Who might rent us a broadcast-quality video camera for the day? The local PBS station? No answer. It's Sunday. What's open?

Although we always used to hand-carry the camera onto the plane, because of increased security and all, we were advised to check the camera in its protective, cushioned case as regular baggage. Somewhere it must have gotten a big bump, and now we're suffering. We do have a mini-DV camera that we use for shooting behind-the-scenes stuff, and that becomes our back-up plan. After much agonizing and Jarrett's making a quick trip back to the motel for the camera's owner's manual, we decide the big camera is not going to function today. Buck and Bob figure out how to get the best possible audio into the little camera, and we proceed to shoot interviews and accompanying pictures at Huong Lan, and it goes reasonably well. We stay much longer than Patrick had hoped, but when we finally stop and have some late lunch, the day doesn't seem to be a disaster at all. We got what we came for: a story and some good *banh mi*.

We fly to Los Angeles early that evening, and by the time we get settled, we settle for convenient (and surprisingly delicious) chicken sandwiches in the hotel's little lobby restaurant. We review our options for renting a camera here, spend some time on the internet checking out various possibilities and equipment lists, and decide we'll get on the phone early tomorrow morning.

Monday August 19 2002
Los Angeles

If you need to rent a not-too-common Beta-SX camera, Los Angeles is probably the best place to be. We find one available, get the insurance stuff we need from Pittsburgh, put the bill on my Visa card, and head for downtown Los Angeles where we're scheduled to spend the day at the legendary Philippe's Original, where the French Dip sandwich is said to have been

born. It's a great place. The food is first-rate, the options of lamb, pork, beef or turkey are all delicious. The mustard is killer hot, and there's communal seating at long tables which means you may be sharing space with strangers if the place is busy, and all these factors make for an decidedly friendly, unusual urban experience. While waiting for the camera to arrive, we eat. We're impressed.

When the rental camera is delivered, it's nearly noon, and we all click into fast-work mode. Buck and Bob and Jarrett try to capture the sights and sounds of the lunchtime rush, Minette and I try to stay out of the shots until we can line up an interview. We tape our talk with Chuck Johnson, the young manager who set up our visit, and he suggests we also chat with his sister, Jeannette Rodenbaugh, and his cousin, Mark Massengill, and they're great, but, as always, some of the best "bites" are from the customers who love this place and all its idiosyncrasies.

Tuesday August 20 2002
Los Angeles to Pittsburgh

Minette, Bob and Jarrett and I fly home to Pittsburgh. Buck is off to Florida, and I promise to call and tell him when I'm coming to Florida to shoot Cuban sandwiches. We also want to get an interview with Dean Young, the man whose father created the "Blondie" comic strip as well as the "Dagwood" sandwich.

Wednesday August 21 2002
WQED Pittsburgh

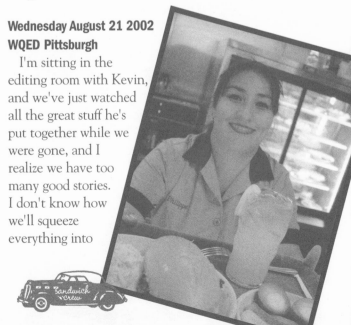

I'm sitting in the editing room with Kevin, and we've just watched all the great stuff he's put together while we were gone, and I realize we have too many good stories. I don't know how we'll squeeze everything into an hour, and I'm trying to schedule the Florida trip, and suddenly it hits me: cancel Florida. I get several extra days of editing and a little less material to cram into the program.

Thursday August 22 - Sunday September 15 2002
WQED Pittsburgh

No time for diary entries. We edit edit edit. I line up the sound bites, write connecting narration, and then Kevin covers the stories with pictures. On September 6, we re-shoot the interviews with Tom and Gail at Isaly's here in Pittsburgh because there were bad problems with the audio from our earlier shoot. We also get shots of some local *banh mi* and a few Primanti's sandwiches in the Strip District here.

I hate that we will have to cut so many good stories and delicious footage.

Wednesday September 18 2002
WQED Pittsburgh

We air a "sneak preview" of the hour-long show for our Pittsburgh audience. The show is in four segments, and we have to tape pledge breaks that will go between the segments, making a total program of almost 90 minutes. Minette and I will do the breaks with our friend Chris Fennimore who is also WQED's director of programming and the host of his own series of cooking shows called America's Home Cooking. He's great on pledge. We're happy that we have to keep the breaks relatively short according to our contract with PBS.

It goes well. During the second and third pledge

breaks, the phones ring non-stop. These pledge breaks will be shown along with the program when it airs on PBS early in 2003. We hope for the best.

Thursday September 19 2002
WQED Pittsburgh

We find out from our ratings service that we got great ratings last night (averaging a 5.5 / 9 if you can read ratings), making us the highest rated program on PBS anywhere in the country last night. Not bad.

Kevin and I still need to finish the 90-minute "DVD version" of the show that will include a lot of extras, including some of the stories that we couldn't squeeze into the program, but the end is near.

Tuesday October 1 2002

I get an email from PBS telling me that our program will air nationally on Wednesday, January 8, 2003. That means we have to have everything to PBS by November 1.

Kevin is ready to drive to Chicago for an Italian beef. Minette is craving lobster rolls. Matt wants a falafel in Watertown. Jarrett says he could go for a Chickie's Special, although Bob says he's been thinking about Katz's pastrami. I often wish I were at Thelma's, and a Maid Rite would be nice, but meanwhile I'm happy to have easy access to the Slammer at Isaly's here in Pittsburgh.

We're all still hungry for sandwiches. That's a good sign.

You can get copies of Rick's programs at www.wqed.org Click on "Shop WQED"

Resources for
Finding Great
Sandwiches

The following is a short list of excellent Internet sites for locating great sandwiches and restaurants in the United States.

http://www.chowhound.com Professional restaurant critic/author Jim Leff and Bob Okomura host this forum for talking about great chow and where to get it.

http://www.HollyEats.com If it's out there and it's good eating, Holly Moore knows about it, and he provides all the details along with his grease stain rating system.

http://www.nj.com/munchmobile Travel to the best eating spots in New Jersey with the *Star-Ledger* Munchmobile crew.

http://www.dixiedining.com "Put some South in your mouth" with Gary Saunders.

http://www.fat-guy.com Stephen A. Shaw's guide to eating in New York City and environs.

http://www.roadfood.com and http://www.splendidtable.org/whereweeat
Catch up with Jane and Michael Stern's latest discoveries at these two sites.

internet reference sites

http://gonewengland.about.com/library/weekly/aa011600a.htm
http://hicards.com/platinum/bizarre/5-6.html
http://icuban.com
http://members.aol.com/acalendar/July/beans.html
http://members.cox.net/jjschnebel/hotdogs.html
http://members.tripod.com/womanola/ybor.html
http://naid.sppsr.ucla.edu/coneyisland/articles/food.htm
http://nola.com/tastes/topten/joints/parasols.html
http://pittsburgh.citysearch.com
http://seafood.ucdavis.edu/pubs/albacorefishery.htm
http://southernfood.about.com/library/weekly/aa060198.htm
http://texascooking.netrelief.com
http://worldwrapps.com
http://www.acmeoyster.com
http://www.bartleby.com
http://www.beeffoodservice.com
http://www.boston-online.com/faq.html
http://www.carseywerner.net/inflight/roseanne/roseanne_904.htm
http://www.chicogohs.org
http://www.digitalcity.com/pittsburgh
http://www.emporia.edu
http://www.ferrarapan.com
http://www.foodreference.com
http://www.geocities.com/etymonline/s13etm.htm
http://www.golfweb.com
http://www.gti.net/mocolib1/kid/foodfaq.html
http://www.gti.net/mocolib1/kid/foodfaq2.html
http://www.gumbopages.com
http://www.hollyeats.com
http://www.hormel.com
http://www.ilovecheese.com
http://www.jamesbeard.org/events/words/eggs_benedict.shtml
http://www.kdhx.org
http://www.kingfeatures.com/features/comics/blondie/aboutMaina.php
http://www.latortillafactory.com
http://www.lessontutor.com/eesPittsburgh.html

http://www.lib.ucdavis.edu/exhibits/food/index.html
http://www.maid-rite.com
http://www.mainelobsterpromo.com
http://www.mineosapio.com
http://www.nppc.org
http://www.outlawcook.com
http://www.patskingofsteaks.com
http://www.peanutbutterlovers.com/history/index.html
http://www.philippes.com
http://www.pittsburghtrivia.com
http://www.pjstar.com/news/restaurants/shenans021700.html
http://www.plainsfolk.com
http://www.porkchopjohns.com
http://www.porktimes.org
http://www.potshopofboston.com/hist.html
http://www.primantibros.com
http://www.tampabayalive.com
http://www.texascooking.com
http://www.todayinsci.com
http://www.tri-cityherald.com/recipes/world/world6.html
http://www.turkeyfed.org
http://www.tvacres.com/food_meats.htm
http://www.umaine.edu/folklife/bhbhistory.htm
http://www.umkc.edu/orgs/kcjazz/jazzspot/clubreno.htm
http://www.underwoodspreads.com
http://www.uni-mainz.de/~pwacker/sandwich.html
http://www.uselessknowledge.com/word/hero.shtml
http://www.visitmayberry.com
http://www.visit-springfieldillinois.com/pressroom/ideas.htm
http://www.visualstore.com
http://www.wawa.com
http://www.whatscookingamerica.net
http://www.wheatfoods.org
http://www.wyes.org
http:// pubindex.lapl.org
http://www.yatcom.com/neworl/dining/parasols523.html

selected bibliography and resources

COOKBOOKS, FOOD REFERENCE PUBLICATIONS, AND PERIODICALS

"A People on the Move: Germans in Russia and in the Former Soviet Union: 1763 – 1997." Stuttgart, Germany: Landsmannschaft der Deutschen aus Russlan e.V., Kulturrat der Deutschen aus Russland e. V., 1997. Translation from German to English by Ingeborg W. Smith, Western Springs, Illinois. http://www.lib.ndsu.nodak.edu/grch/history_culture/history/people.html

Aidells, Bruce and Denis Kelly. *Bruce Aidells' Complete Sausage Book*. Berkeley, CA: Ten Speed Press, 2000.

_____. *Hot Links and Country Flavors*. New York: Alfred A. Knopf, 1990.

_____. *Real Beer and Good Eats*. New York: Alfred A. Knopf, 1992.

Anderson, Jean. *The American Century Cookbook*. New York: Clarkson Potter, 1997.

Beard, James. *James Beard's American Cookery*. Boston: Little, Brown & Company, 1972.

Beckwith, Chet. *Too Good To Be True*. Baton Rouge, LA: Self-published, 1992.

Berman, Eleanor. *New York Neighborhoods*. Guilford, CT: The Globe Pequot Press, 2001.

Brobeck, Florence. *The Lunch Box and Every Kind of Sandwich*. New York: Greystone Press, 1946.

Brown, Helen Evans. *West Coast Cook Book*. Boston: Little, Brown & Company, 1952.

Bruno, Pat. *Chicago's Food Favorites: A Guide to More Than 450 Favorite Eating Spots*. Chicago: Contemporary Books, Inc., 1986.

_____. Email correspondence, June 22, 2002.

_____. "Sandwiches Are Choice Cuban Imports." http://www.suntimes.com, March 1, 2002.

Bulla, David. "Chicken Fried Steak – A Texas Tradition Revisited." http://www.texascooking.com, June, 2002.

Burnett, Arlene. "Kitchen Mailbox: Turkey Devonshire Sandwich Still a Classic Pittsburgh Original." http://www.post-gazette.com, February 15, 2001.

Crone, Thomas. "The Seven Deadly Sins, II: Gluttony and the St. Paul Sandwich." http://www.stltoday.com, December 28, 2001.

Dabney, Joseph T. *Smokehouse Ham, Spoon Bread, & Scuppernong Wine*. Nashville, TN: Cumberland House, 1998.

De' Medici, Lorenza and Fred Plotkin. *Italy Today: The Beautiful Cookbook*. New York: HarperCollins Publishers, Inc., 1997.

Dilg, Marie. "The Secret's in the Sauce." http://www.companysj.com/v161/sauce.html

Dinner, S.P. "Investors Purchase Maid-Rite Chain." http://desmoinesregister.com, April 6, 2002.

Duff, Gail. *A Loaf of Bread: Bread in History, in the Kitchen, and on the Table*. Edison, NJ: Chartwell Books, Inc., 1998.

Dull, Mrs. S.R. *Southern Cooking*. New York: Grosset & Dunlap, Inc., 1928, 1968.

Edge, John T. *A Gracious Plenty*. New York: G.P. Putnam's Sons, 1999.

_____. *Southern Belly*. Athens, GA: Hill Street Press, 2000.

Editors of American Heritage. *The American Heritage Cookbook and Illustrated History of American Eating & Drinking*. New York: American Heritage Publishing Co., Inc., 1964.

Egerton, John. *Southern Food: At Home, on the Road, in History*. Chapel Hill, NC: The University of North Carolina Press, 1993.

Ehler, Chef James T. *Food Reference Website*. http://www.foodreference.com

Farmer, Fannie Merritt. *The Original Boston Cooking-School Cook Book*. Hugh Lauter Levin Associates, Inc., a facsimile of the first edition, 1896, 1996.

Flemmons, Jerry. *Plowboys, Cowboys and Slanted Pigs*. Fort Worth, TX: Texas Christian University Press, 1984.

Flexner, Marion. *Out of Kentucky Kitchens*. New York: Bramhall House, 1949.

Fuller, Eva Greene. *The Up-to-date Sandwich Book: 400 Ways to Make a Sandwich*. Chicago: A. C. McClurg & Co., 1909.

Gee, Denise. "The Rich Life of the Po'Boy." http://www.coastalliving.com/seafood/poboy/poboy.asp

Hale, William Harlan and The Editors of Horizon Magazine. *The Horizon Cookbook and Illustrated History of Eating and Drinking through the Ages*. American Heritage Publishing Co., Inc., 1968.

Harmon, John E. "The Spiedie – a Tasty Morsel." http://www.geography.ccsu.edu/harmonj/atlas/spiedie.htm

Hawkins, Nancy and Arthur. *The American Regional Cookbook*. Englewood Cliffs, NJ: Prentice-Hall, Inc., 1976.

Heyhoe, Kate. "Remembering the Sandwich: Great Moments, Great Sandwiches in History." http://www.globalgourmet.com/food/kgk051901.html

Hill, Annabella P. *Mrs. Hill's Southern Practical Cookery and Receipt Book*. Columbia, SC: University of South Carolina Press, 1867, 1870, 1995.

Hudson, Roger. Email correspondence, May, 2002.

_____. "Gittin' Back to My Roots," http://www.epinions.com, October 5, 2001.

Jones, Evan. *American Food: The Gastronomic Story*. Woodstock, NY: The Overlook Press, 1990.

Kontzer, Tony. "Falafel's a San Jose Melting Pot." Silicon Valley/San Jose Business Journal, July 1, 1996.

Leslie, Eliza. *Miss Leslie's Directions for Cookery – An Unabridged Reprint of the 1851 Classic*. Mineola, NY: Dover Publications, 1999.

Lincoln, Mrs. D.A. *Boston Cooking School Cook Book: A Reprint of the 1884 Classic*. Mineola, NY: Dover Publications, Inc., 1996.

Lovegren, Sylvia. *Fashionable Food*. New York: MacMillan, 1995.

Lowney, Pamela. "Local Flavor: Brain, the Other White Meat." http://www.stltoday.com, February 12, 2002.

Mariani, John. *The Encyclopedia of American Food & Drink*. New York: Lebhar-Friedman Books, 1999.

Merriman, Woodene. "A High Point for Venerable Restaurant Family." http://www.post-gazette.com, April 13, 1999.

Miller, Gloria Bley. *The Thousand Chinese Recipe Cookbook*. New York: Portland House, 1997.

Nathan, Joan. *Jewish Cooking in America*. New York: Alfred A. Knopf, 1996.

_____. *The Foods of Israel Today*. New York: Alfred A. Knopf, 2001.

Nickles, Harry G. and the Editors of Time-Life Books. *Middle Eastern Cooking*. New York: Time-Life Books, 1969.

O'Neill, Molly. *New York Cookbook*. New York: Workman Publishing, 1992.

Otto, Steve. "Those Yankees Need to Stick to the Deli." http://tampatrib.com, Feb. 10, 2002.

Penny, Prudence. *Coupon Cookery*. Hollywood, CA: Murray & Gee, Inc., 1943

Pillsbury, Richard. *No Foreign Food: The American Diet in Time and Place*. Boulder, CO: Westview Press, 1998.

Poole, Marcia. "Enterprising Family Makes Dining Fun." http://www.trib.com, April 14, 1996.

Porterfield, James D. *Dining by Rail*. New York: St. Martin's Griffin, 1993.

_____. Email correspondence, August, 2002.

Rader, Jim. "American Food Folklore and Culinary History: Buffalo Wings, Reuben Sandwiches, and Caesar Salads." http://www.uta.fi/FAST/US8/SPEC/foodfolk.html

Randolph, Mary. *The Virginia House-wife*. Columbia, SC: University of South Carolina Press, 1824, facsimile edition 1984.

Root, Waverly and Richard de Rochemont. *Eating in America*. New York: William Morrow and Company, Inc., 1976.

Rose, Pat." It's a Wrap for Wrap Works." http://www.noevalleyvoice.com, November, 1998.

Rutledge, Sarah. *The Carolina Housewife, A Facsimile of the 1847 Edition*. Columbia, SC: University of South Carolina Press.

Ryan, Ellen. Special to the Washington Post, http://www.broadcast.net/~sbe1/history/spiedies.html, January 17, 2001.

Santiago, Fabiola. "A Politically Correct Sandwich: The Elena Ruz Has No Castro Link." The Miami Herald, August 15, 1996.

Smith, Andrew F. Peanuts: *The Illustrious History of the Goober Pea*. Urbana and Chicago, IL: University of Illinois Press, 2002.

Smith, Grace and Beverly and Charles Morrow Wilson. *Through the Kitchen Door: A Cook's Tour to the Best Kitchens of America*. New York: Stackpole Sons, 1938.

Smith, Jeff. *The Frugal Gourmet On Our Immigrant Ancestors*. New York: William Morrow and Company, Inc., 1990.

Staff of the Brown Derby Restaurants. *The Brown Derby Cookbook*. Garden City, NY: Doubleday & Company, Inc., 1949.

Stern, Jane and Michael. *Blue Plate Specials & Blue Ribbon Chefs*. New York: Lebhar-Friedman Books, 2001.

_____. *Eat Your Way Across the U.S.A.* New York: Broadway Books, 1999.

_____. "The Un-Burger", Gourmet, August, 2002.

Storrow, Amy. "Sub Species," Saveur, Issue No. 53.

Swearengen, Anita. "Critique: C & K Barbecue." http://www.saucecafe.com

Tartan, Beth. *North Carolina & Old Salem Cookery*. Chapel Hill, NC: The University of North Carolina Press, 1955, 1992.

The American Heritage Cookbook and Illustrated History of American Eating & Drinking. New York: American Heritage Publishing, 1964.

The Browns, Cora, Rose, and Bob. *America Cooks: Favorite Recipes from the 48 States*. Garden City, NY: Garden City Publishing Company, Inc., 1940.

The Home Institute of the New York Herald Tribune. *Young America's Cookbook: A Cook Book for Boys and Girls Who Like Good Food*. New York: Charles Scribner's Sons, 1944.

The Melting Pot: Ethnic Cuisine in Texas. San Antonio, TX: The University of Texas Institute of Texan Cultures at San Antonio, 1989.

Thompson, Terry. *Cajun-Creole Cooking*. Tucson, AZ: HPBooks, 1986.

Thorne, John and Matt. "Bahn Mi and Me," Simple Cooking, May/June, 1999.

Thomas, Marvin. "Springfield's Only Tabarin Bares the City's Soul." http://www.llcc.cc.il.us/harvest/resilmar.htm, Summer, 1995.

Three Guys From Miami™. *Cuban Food with Attitude*. Musibay, Lindgren and Castillo, LLP, E-book, 2001, 2002.

Tyree, Marion Cabell. *Housekeeping in Old Virginia*. Louisville, KY: Favorite Recipes Press, 1879, facsimile edition 1965.

Vietnamese sandwich history/origins post. http://www.chowhound.com/boards,crave/messages/8763.html March 8, 2002.

Villas, James. *American Taste*. New York: Arbor House, 1982.

Voltz, Jeanne. *The California Cookbook*. Indianapolis, IN: The Bobbs-Merrill Company, Inc., 1970

_____ and Caroline Stuart. *The Florida Cookbook*. New York: Alfred A. Knopf, 1993.

Wakefield, Ruth. *Toll House Tried and True Recipes*. New York: M. Barrows & Company, Inc., 1943.

Walsh, Robb. "Chicken-Fried Honor." http://www.houstonpress.com/issues/2001-01-11/café.html, January 11, 2001.

Witzel, Michael Karl. *The American Drive-In Restaurant*. St. Paul, MN: MBI Publishing Company, 1994, 2002.

Wyman, Carolyn. *I'm a SPAM Fan*. Stamford, CT: Longmeadow Press, 1993.

Young, Chic. *Blondie's Cook Book*. Philadelphia, PA: David McKay Company, 1947.

Zeldes, Leah A. "How to Eat Like a Chicagoan." http://diningchicago.com, September 19, 2000.

index

notes